Pedagogy of the Oppress*or*

Pedagogy of the Oppress*or*

Experiential Education on the US/Mexico Border

Jerry H. Gill

RESOURCE *Publications* · Eugene, Oregon

PEDAGOGY OF THE OPPRESSOR
Experiential Education on the US/Mexico Border

Resource Publications
An Imprint of Wipf and Stock Publishers
199 W. 8th Ave., Suite 3
Eugene, OR 97401

www.wipfandstock.com

PAPERBACK ISBN: 978-1-6667-2020-4
HARDCOVER ISBN: 978-1-6667-2000-6
EBOOK ISBN: 978-1-6667-2001-3

09/16/21

For
Rick Ufford-Chase
Founder, Director, and Energizer of BorderLinks
And
Most of all, a Great Friend and Teacher

Contents

A Matter of Perspective

Raising Consciousness and Conscience

MANY READERS OF THESE pages will recognize the play on words indicated in the title of the book. Paulo Freire's very well-known work *Pedagogy of the Oppressed* sought to justify and expound his own theories about education in relation to the oppression that people of the developing countries encounter largely as a result of the economic and political exploitation imposed by dominating countries of the so called developed world. The title of this present work is meant to call attention to the parallel need for a pedagogy for the people of this latter, privileged class, the oppressors.

The format for the explorations in the present volume will largely follow Freire's own outline, but in a somewhat inverted fashion. Whereas Freire focused on the education of those who are oppressed, this book focuses on those who do the oppressing. Thus many of the issues and techniques introduced by Freire will be reversed or inverted when applied to the education of the oppressor class. Obviously this sort of transposition technique can only be applied in a flexible manner since the conditions comprising the contexts of the two sides of the equation are quite different. Others of Freire's insights and analyses will remain relevant to the discussion, but will be reinterpreted so as to be pertinent to the other side of the equation.

In addition, the problems and principles discussed in these explorations will be illustrated by drawing from the vision and experience of an organization named BorderLinks, which has offered experiential education opportunities on the US/Mexico border for many years. Of course, these concrete examples constitute but one approach to the issues at hand. Nevertheless, this approach has proven to be a highly useful one for many, many individuals and groups over the years since 1987. In fact, for a few years BorderLinks had an average of one thousand people annually through its various programs. In addition, the organization grew a great deal in size, both with respect to facilities and staff. The campus in Nogales, Sonora, Mexico became a large-scale community center that provided lunch every school day for over two hundred children and offered a wide variety of recreational and educational programs as well.

BorderLinks provides three basic sorts of educational experiences for North Americans along the US/Mexican border centering in Nogales, Sonora. The first involves one to three week travel seminars for church groups, college students, and seminarians. The second is a regular semester on the border for undergraduates in connection with a number of colleges and universities around the United States. The third educational program takes the form of occasional bi-national conferences on various border issues such as economics, health and environment, and immigration. In addition, BorderLinks entered into partnership with Catholic Relief Services to provide small loans to individual Mexicans to enable them to start up fledgling businesses of their own.

As a bi-national organization at its height, BorderLinks was led by two directors, one in Nogales Sonora, the other in Tucson, Arizona, with a campus in each of these cities. The U.S. director was Rick Ufford-Chase, who founded the organization in 1987. The Mexican director was Francisco Trujillo. There were about twenty-five bi-lingual staff members who performed a variety of tasks from leading travel seminars to raising funds and managing the offices to teaching courses. Three of the Mexican staff were Madres of the Sacred Order of the Eucharist, based in Colima, Mexico. There was also a bi-national Board of Directors that oversaw the entire operation, as well as numerous volunteer supporters on both sides of the border.

The examples considered in the course of the following discussion of Paulo Freire's principles as applied to the process of educating those of us living a privileged life will be taken from the experiences of the Border-Links organization. Hopefully these examples will provide a concrete and human dimension to the exploration of the educational and political theories involved in actually seeking to make North Americans aware of border realities. There are, to be sure, other approaches and examples that could be discussed, but these should be sufficient to make the following explorations concrete and to the point.

The educational process around which Paulo Freire's work centers is generally referred to as *consciousness raising*. Of course this notion has been used for some time now in regard to the idea of effecting a major alteration in a person's understanding of a given reality. In theoretic discourse today it has been augmented by the expression 'paradigm shift' in order to refer to a significant broadening of one's perspective or the conceptual framework within which one experiences any aspect of the world.

Freire's basic concern is with enabling oppressed people to come to an understanding of their socio-political situation so as to be able to become active participants in the process of its development. This sort of understanding is not the sort of thing that can simply be explained or taught to someone as a piece of information or new idea, because it involves a new way of seeing or experiencing from a different and/or more encompassing perspective. It is sometimes compared to altering the horizon within which one experiences the whole of reality itself.

The most common contexts to which this notion has been applied in recent years are those surrounding such issue as racism and feminism. It is generally explained that our way of seeing the world is determined by traditional stereotypes concerning people of races other than our own and of women's roles in society, thus calling for the need to transform the very lenses through which we have come to experience and thus think about these realities. One's awareness or consciousness gets raised to a higher level of understanding. This sort of consciousness raising or paradigm shifting can also be seen in the fields of science, politics, art, and religion. Einsteinian physics fundamentally altered the way we think about outer space, even as Copernican astronomy altered our way of conceiving of our solar system. Egalitarian and democratic concepts of government radically challenged those of monarchies, as did renaissance and impressionistic modes of painting with respect to previous ways of seeing and experiencing the world. Similar shifts in consciousness with respect to pantheism, polytheism, and monotheism, for example, can be noted in the fields of religion and theology.

Freire's contention is that severely oppressed people do not generally experience life or see themselves as oppressed or as capable of effecting change in their own everyday world. A consciousness raising process is thus required for them to truly understand and begin to participate in their own socio-political situation. This is not a function of any traditional educational methodology, but is rather the hoped for outcome of specific, yet indirect ways of bringing people to a place from which they can see their reality and their place in it in a fresh way.

In like manner, the task of effecting consciousness raising among those of us who live a privileged existence and are unaware of the oppression this existence causes in the lives of people in the developing countries is far from easy. Here as well the job is not one of simple explanation or of offering or transferring information. Rather, it involves creating an experiential arena within which North Americans can interact with those persons living as oppressed people.

Specifically, the task on the US/Mexico border is that of bringing North Americans into direct contact with Mexican people along the border in their homes, streets, and places of work so they can encounter the realities of their existence in something of a first-hand manner. This involves a great deal of time consuming work arranging for visits to *maquiladoras*, or assembly plants, homestays with families in *colonias*, or squatter neighborhoods, and meetings with various agencies like the border patrol, immigration officers, and migrant centers. There also are books and papers to be read, as well as actual work to be done alongside the people who are living this reality.

In the midst of all this activity BorderLinks educators also schedule times for visiting groups to reflect on and discuss their experiences. Indeed, since BorderLinks is an ecumenical faith-based organization, a good deal of this time is frequently devoted to a consideration of the religious and theological implications of the realities being encountered. It is in these reflection sessions that the seeds of consciousness raising are introduced into the minds and hearts of the North American participants.

One of the primary techniques for focusing such reflections is to consider a specific biblical passage, usually from the New Testament gospels, in which Jesus engages people of differing cultural backgrounds and faith perspectives. The characters in these Bible stories each have different needs and experiences that often parallel those of oppressed people today, since they too live in a time and place of great socio-political oppression under the imperialism of the Roman Empire. Discussion of these passages is always open and unforced, with participants being encouraged to relate the text to their own experience, as well as that of the people they are meeting along the border.

The educational process integral to such consciousness raising is frequently described in terms of a three-fold formula, "See, reflect, act." This formula arose out of the Young Christian Worker movement in Belgium in the middle of the twentieth century and became an unspoken guideline for both the Second Vatican Council and the theology of liberation that has shaped Latin American religious thought and life during the last fifty years. The basic idea behind this formula, which is often used to summarize the thought of both Paulo Freire and Gustavo Gutierrez, the leading theologian of the liberation theological movement, is that all true learning begins with an encounter with the actual realities under consideration. It is first necessary to actually see or experience life as lived by oppressed people. Only then can one engage in reflective thought and discussion about the significance of these realities, a process that is every bit as necessary as that of seeing them. Finally, then, one is in a position to act and respond to the situation at hand in a responsible manner.

It must be acknowledged that this three-fold pattern is a cyclical one in which each cycle leads again to yet another, in an on-going fashion. Moreover, the three phases actually interpenetrate one another since in some way each presupposes and informs the others. To think or act without first seeing leads to empty thought or blind activism, while only to see without reflecting or acting results in quietism and apathy. True understanding involves experience, thought, and action. Only by incorporating each of these dimensions of cognition is consciousness raising possible, whether for the oppressed or for the oppressor.

The reader may already have noticed that the terms consciousness raising in English and Spanish, as well as Portuguese, are based on the same linguistic stem as the word 'conscience.' It should mentioned that this is no accident. In fact, in Portuguese and Spanish both mental and moral awareness are designated by the same term. It is an unfortunate development in the English language that these two forms of awareness have been separated. We in North America generally do not associate consciousness with morality, since for us it is quite possible for a person to be conscious of something without feeling or taking any responsibility for it.

For this reason it must be stressed at the outset that the sort of consciousness raising being envisioned and practiced by both Paulo Freire and BorderLinks involves the integration of what we North Americans generally regard as two different and distinct aspects of human experience. However, to actually see some feature or dimension of a situation, to be aware of it in concrete reality, would seem to entail that one is also engaged with it on a moral level. To have one's consciousness raised is, one would think, at the same time to have one's conscience raised as well. Unfortunately, this is not always the case.

A specific example of how this integrated dynamic can and should work is found in the life and activity of the now famous Bishop Samuel Ruiz, who began his ministry in Chiapas, Mexico with the mindset of a typical European trained cleric over forty years ago. However, after actually seeing the exploited and oppressed lives of the native people in Latin America, and reflecting on them in relation to the scriptures and the Second Vatican Council, Bishop Ruiz completely altered the direction of his work so as to incorporate their experience, needs, and perspective. His conscience had been transformed because his consciousness had been raised.

BorderLinks specifically seeks to go to special lengths to see to it that the participants in its programs have ample opportunity to experience the realities of the US/Mexico border for themselves. This does not mean that BorderLinks is a value free organization. It simply means that both participants and those who direct the various educational activities share a common experience and engage in honest dialogue with one another concerning it. A serious effort is made to allow the lives of those living on the border to speak for themselves—and to allow those who have come to learn about the border to do so for themselves as well.

Finally, let me bring this introduction to a close by offering a few pieces of historical information that can serve as a backdrop for understanding what the US/Mexico border is and how it came to be what it is today. We North Americans by and large know very little about the border that separates us and Mexican people from each other. This in large part explains why we actually care so little about how the border impacts the lives of those living along it. Both fortunately and unfortunately the difficulties at the border have reached such gigantic proportions that we can no longer ignore them, and the US government has finally begun to worry about what to do about the situation.

In the late 1840s the United States fought a war with Mexico over exactly where the boundary between the two countries was to lie. The state of Texas's struggle for independence played a significant role in this war, as well. In 1848 a treaty was signed, called the Treaty of Guadalupe-Hidalgo, and the border was established along the Rio Grande river and extending westward through New Mexico, Arizona, and California. A glance at a map will show that the US acquired about one quarter of the current continental United States, while Mexico lost about one third of its previous land in this settlement.

A few years later, when the US wanted to extend the railroad system across the Southwest, it arranged to relocate the Western part of the border about hundred miles further south across Arizona and New Mexico. Thus many Mexican people whose families lived for hundreds of years along what is now the border are fond of saying: "I am Mexican, but I did not cross the border, the border crossed me." It should not go unmentioned that this whole episode cost Mexico a great many lives and the US a relatively small amount of money. This deal is generally referred to as the Gadsden Purchase since it was carried out by a US diplomat named Gadsden.

The people living on the northern side of this new border were assured by the US government that they would now be full-fledged American citizens and would be able to keep their land and vote. Unfortunately, this did not happen because land developers and various government agencies soon swindled these folks out of their lands by taking advantage of their lack of knowledge of the laws and the English language. Thus a corridor of second-class citizens was created along the border known today as the Latino or Chicano subculture. A great number of people then became and still remain disenfranchised from their land, from good schools, and from adequate employment.

For many years things remained pretty much the same along the Mexican side of the border, with folks crossing back and forth easily for both work and family visits. In the late 1960s US companies began to place factories and assembly plants along the Mexican side of the border because the rent and labor were extremely cheap. Many folks began to move from central Mexico to work in these factories because their family and co-operative farms were unable to compete with the big agro-business companies. This relocation process began to tear the fabric of Mexican social life.

Beginning in the 1990s this relocation process moved into high gear because more and more US companies established their assembly plants, called 'maquiladoras,' along the border on the Mexican side. Parts for everything from pants and jackets to electronic equipment began to be shipped across the border into the US, assembled for about one dollar an hour, labelled *Made in the USA*, and sold for inexpensive prices in stores like Wal-Mart. At last count there were over 3000 of these plants along the Mexican side of the border, with the number still growing with no end in sight. In 1994 the North American Free Trade Agreement (NAFTA) essentially guaranteed that goods and money could continue to move freely across the border, but Mexican laborers cannot. Recent changes in the NAFTA agreement have not substantially altered this pattern.

The incredible population explosion in cities like Ciudad Juarez, directly across the Rio Grande from El Paso, Texas, and the twin cities of Nogales in Mexico and Arizona, has created unbelievable social and economic problems because there are so few social facilities for the literally hundreds of thousands of people who have migrated northward. Most of these folks live in squatter villages without electricity, running water, and sewage, to say nothing of paved streets, schools, and hospitals. Working conditions in most of the *maquiladoras* are fairly adequate, but the terribly low wages, usually a dollar per hour, make it necessary for every member of a family to work full-time just to keep their heads above the survival line. The cost of living on the Mexican side of the border is about 75 percent of that on the US side, and yet a family must spend 70 percent of its income on food because the wages are so low. In addition, no health or retirement benefits are provided by the US owned assembly plants. Moreover, most employees are young women, and if they get pregnant they are let go.

The current situation has been greatly compounded, especially since the events of September 11, 2001 by the US government's efforts to tighten border control and greatly increasing the number of border patrol agents and electronic detection equipment. The militarization of the border has forced those seeking asylum in the US to try to sneak across the border in highly dangerous desert regions where every year hundreds of people die in the process of crossing. All of these issues were exacerbated during the Trump Administration. Undocumented Mexican immigrants seeking asylum now number at least eleven million. The US immigration laws stand in need of drastic revamping but there is little hope of this happening in the immediate future.

Taken together, then, the two sides of the border constitute a unique third country which is neither in the United States or Mexico, it is *la frontera*, the borderlands. It is this reality that BorderLinks seeks to educate US citizens about by providing experiential educational opportunities to raise consciousness and transform lives. It seeks, then, to provide a small but hopefully powerful beginning for the pedagogy of the oppressor. These opportunities at times actually include direct interaction with the migrants crossing the border in the desert in order to learn about their experience more fully. This border may well be the only place on the planet where the developed and the developing worlds meet, and thus it is an excellent classroom in which to learn about the globalization processes that are redefining the world, a place to see, reflect, and prepare for action.

This then is a brief introduction to the central notion at the heart of the pedagogical process envisioned by both Paulo Freire and the BorderLinks organization. Although the particular dynamics involved in the education of the oppressed and the oppressors necessarily differ in something of the reverse order, the cognitive process is essentially the same in both cases. A fresh way of viewing and understanding the world and one's place in it is what is involved, and a radical transformation of one's own life is the result.

It is, to be sure, important to recognize that no educational endeavor takes place in a vacuum, that all knowledge is what is today called situated knowledge. Thus there are socio-political aspects involved in all cognition, consciousness raising included. At one end of the spectrum there are efforts at pure indoctrination wherein all previous knowledge is supposedly expunged from the subject's mind. At the other extreme are the claims of so called pure science wherein the knowledge involved is supposed to be absolutely value free. In actuality, neither of these approaches can be realized, since coincidental and human limitations always play an important part.

Nevertheless, there is still a difference between more and less objectivity, where it is clear to those who know and care about the reality under consideration what is and what is not the case. Freire and others, like BorderLinks, who engage in consciousness raising are occasionally accused of forcing their own ideas on those whom they seek to educate. While this is always a danger to be guarded against, and every effort needs to be made to minimize this dynamic, the goal of transformation can be achieved without violating the integrity of the persons involved. If this were not possible, no education whatsoever would ever take place. The effectiveness of the BorderLinks style program speaks for itself.

To return then to initial remarks of this introduction, the aim of this book is to explore the dynamics of educating highly privileged people who, largely unwittingly, contribute substantially to the oppression of people of the developing world. The format will be to present the insights of Paulo Freire as introduced in his book *Pedagogy of the Oppressed* as they might apply, albeit in reversed fashion, to the task of raising the consciousness of those who live in wealthy and dominating North America. Concrete examples of how these insights have and are being incorporated into such a process will be drawn from the vision and practice of the BorderLinks organization.

It needs to be borne in mind that this is an exploratory endeavor. The issues and problems confronted are in no wise simple, and there are more than one or two ways to see them, as well as to work with them. Freire's work itself is not beyond criticism[1] nor is the BorderLinks model the only viable way to apply those insights. Nevertheless, it is important to offer a concrete point of departure for an examination of Freire's insights as they might pertain to working with North Americans in relation to the realities of the US/Mexico border. The focal conviction for the following investigations is that education is the most honorable and persuasive means of effecting significant change both in the world at large and in individual lives. It may be slow, and it may not always work, but it surely ranks higher than the chief alternatives, such as violent revolution, on the one hand, and the continuation of oppression, on the other.

A final word of introduction. It is very difficult to know what terminology to use when referring to the countries involved in border issues. I do not like "Third/First World," nor "developed/underdeveloped," so I will try to avoid such loaded terms as much as possible. Hopefully I am able to find my way around them most of the time. I trust the reader will abide my various alternatives.

1. Berger, *Pyramids*, 111–16.

Chapter One

The Paradoxes of Oppression

BEFORE GETTING UNDERWAY ON our exploration of the possibilities and problems inherent within the notion of a pedagogy of the oppressor, it will prove useful to consider a number of paradoxes attendant to the idea itself. In doing so it will be helpful to introduce these paradoxes in the manner that Freire himself takes them up, but not in the same order.

1. Who Educates Whom?

Freire makes it quite clear from the outset that in the education of the op-pressed it is crucial that those who still do a great deal of the teaching will be oppressed themselves. Although this seems paradoxical in relation to traditional understandings of the pedagogical process, it makes a great deal of sense when one is engaged in the education of oppressed people for the simple reason that unless one begins where the learners actually live, think, and feel, everything will be wasted at best and detrimental at worst.

Here is how Freire himself puts it: "The pedagogy of the oppressed, which is the pedagogy of people engaged in the fight for their liberation, has its roots here. And those who recognize, or begin to recognize themselves as oppressed must be among the developers of this pedagogy. No pedagogy which is truly liberating can remain distant from the oppressed by treating them as unfortunates and by presenting for their emulation models from among the oppressors. The oppressed must be their own example in the struggle for their redemption."[1]

This approach to education only seems wrong-headed when one assumes that learners, especially oppressed peoples, are incapable of contributing to their own education and need to be taught everything they need to know by someone who already knows it. Aside from the likes of Socrates, John Dewey, and a few others, nearly the entire history of education in Western culture has made this assumption and proceeded accordingly. This is not the place to enter into a detailed critique of this approach to education, but suffice it to say that at least in the case of working with oppressed peoples it is necessary to begin where they themselves exist.

If, on the other hand, one begins by assuming that those with whom one is working are not only capable of contributing to their own education, but in fact stand in the unique position for understanding their own situation, then one is in a good position to actually make this possibility a reality. Such a posture presupposes that oppressed people are also capable of rational thought and action. As Freire puts it: "It is necessary to trust in the oppressed and in their ability to reason. Whoever lacks this trust will fail (or will abandon) dialogue, reflection, and communication."[2]

The attitude with which one approaches the pedagogical process is particularly relevant within a political context, for what Karl Marx said about religion being the opiate of the masses applies with equal force to education when it is based on classicist assumptions. If there is nothing to be learned from the oppressed, then any education given to them will just be a device to keep them in their place. Indeed, it is arguable that the vast majority of education provided by Western colonial powers for the people in developing lands has always done precisely that, and today we are all suffering from the fall-out resulting from this approach to education. As the old adage puts it, we generally have sought to provide people with fish rather than teaching them to fish for themselves.

The simple fact of the matter is that oppressed people are oppressed people precisely because others, the rich and powerful, have always been in a position to control them and dictate to them what is "best for them." Thus whenever anyone today seeks to assist the oppressed it is of paramount importance not to repeat this time-worn pattern of telling them how it is with them and what they need to do to change their situation. It is essential to

1. Freire, *Pedagogy*, 53–54.
2. Freire, *Pedagogy*, 66.

begin by allowing the oppressed to speak for themselves, even if this is time consuming and awkward because of their unfamiliarity with the process. It is time to begin by asking those we wish to help what they themselves think they need and want.

When he endeavored to take the teachings of Vatican II seriously in his ministry among the people of Chiapas, Bishop Samuel Ruiz put the above principle into operation. He sought to learn the languages of the indigenous peoples of the area and ceased to use Spanish and/or Latin as the chief language of the church. In addition, Don Samuel began to take the beliefs and practices of the indigenous religions seriously because he agreed with Pope John the 23rd when he said that "the seeds of the Gospel" are already inherent in the native cultures. Finally he listened to the people express their needs and concerns as they experienced them, not as the church and others saw them.

Along with this notion that teachers can learn from those whom they are attempting teach, about how they see and experience their own lives, goes the more radical idea that learners can actually teach their teachers things that the teachers do not as yet know. Oppressed people may not only know things their oppressors do not, but their overall perspective is, in fact, often more inclusive than that of their oppressors because they experience both sides of the fence, as it were, while the ruling class generally only knows its own side of the fence.

Back in the 1960s there was a deep and humorous book entitled *Puttin' on Ole Massa* in which an elderly black mammy revealed a great many ways black people in the south were able to fool their white owners or bosses. The basic idea of the book was that because black slaves and workers lived within the white culture, both as maids and servants, they were in a position to know a great deal about white folks from the inside, as it were. The other side of this truth is that white folks really knew very little, nor did they care, about the lives of the black folk living among them. In this way, the so called "learners" may well have had a good deal to teach their "teachers."

There is a sense, then, in which those who are oppressed may know more about both sides of the great divide between rich and poor, between oppressed and oppressor, because they exist on the bottom side of the equation. Thus they experience both sides of the dynamic, while those who live on the upper side of the hierarchy only experience their own side. This may be part of what liberation theologian Gustavo Gutierrez means by the phrase the "preferential option for the poor." The experience and perspective of the oppressed is not preferred because they are better or wiser than their oppressors, but because their view is less narrow than theirs, and therefore provides a preferred point of view.

Therefore, as Freire says: "A revolutionary leadership must accordingly practice co-intentional education. Teachers and students (leadership and people), co-intent on reality, are both Subjects . . . In this way the presence of the oppressed in the struggle for their liberation will be what it should be: not pseudo-participation, but committed involvement."[3] Thus the definition of what constitutes a learner and a teacher, respectively, needs to be seen as involving a symbiotic relationship, rather than one in which the person who is thought to be superior, perhaps by those on both sides of the equation, functions as the dispenser of knowledge.

When it comes to putting these insights into practice on the US/Mexican border, BorderLinks seeks to begin with the reality of the people living and working there, letting them speak for themselves. This to be sure is much easier said than done, but for the most part it seems to have become a reality. In addition to striving to be a bi-national organization by systematically seeking staff members as well as board members who represent a Mexican perspective, BorderLinks has continually worked at grounding its vision and programs in people and projects that arise from and speak to the needs of the oppressed along the border. Indeed, when it first began to work in Mexico BorderLinks refused to try to change anything, but instead insisted on first getting to know the local people in their own physical, social, and economic environment.

Right from the first the primary focus was on finding ways to put North Americans in direct contact and dialogue with people living on the border, in their homes, *colonias*, and places of employment. At the heart of every travel seminar lay meals and/or overnight stays with extremely disenfranchised families. During these visits the hosts are asked to tell the story of how they came to the border and what has happened to them since then. Guests are encouraged to ask questions as well, and these could often turn out to be as enlightening as they are sometimes naïve.

Nearly every trip to the border also includes a visit to a *maquiladora*, or assembly plant, so the delegates can see firsthand what the working conditions are. It is always a bit tricky to arrange these visits because the managers are often suspicious as to the motives of the visitors. Whenever possible

3. Freire, *Pedagogy*, 69.

BorderLinks staff members try to arrange for delegates to talk with specific workers as well as with supervisors and managers. Obviously, the points of view expressed by these two quite different perspectives are often contrary to each other, and this can be highly educational. Moreover, delegations are frequently pleasantly surprised to see that the working conditions in these assembly plants are not straight out of a Charles Dickens novel.

On the occasion of one of the home visits a group of some twenty five persons was crowded into a two room home with dirt floors, being served dinner in candle light by a single mother of five. After listening to the woman tell her story and recount her difficulties in trying to purchase her home as well as feed her family, one of the guests asked her what it is that gives her hope. Without a trace of self-pity or dramatic effect the woman answered: "Hope is a luxury that I do without. I simply get up every morning and go to work." It is difficult for North Americans to imagine living without hope.

What is truly amazing about the educational experience one receives from people living on the border in absolutely dire circumstances is, in fact, their great faith and hope. When my wife and I participated in our first BorderLinks trip, we stayed with a family that had five children living in two rooms, also with dirt floors, an outside kitchen and an outhouse. We ate beans and tortillas nearly every meal. The father worked construction and the eldest daughter worked in a *maquiladora*. Nevertheless, these folks were not the least bit bitter about their situation. They were glad to be working and obviously shared a great deal of love and laughter with each other, as well as with us.

When one actually meets and interacts with people who are oppressed it is possible to learn a lot about their lives and of one's own, as well as about what makes the world go around. As Gustavo Gutierrez frequently says, to be in solidarity with the poor and oppressed is to learn how to see reality from a different, more well-rounded perspective. The lives of such people can actually teach those of us living the luxury of the "developed" world a great deal, not only about their difficulties and poverty, but about what values are really worth holding for—and about what really is valuable in life. So often people in oppressed countries have far more love, faith, grace, and hope than those of us living in oppressive countries.

Gutierrez reminds us of how important it is to actually spend time with the poor, accompanying them in the day to day journey in order to get some concrete sense of what life is really like for those at the bottom of the pecking order. This fits with the familiar adage about the necessity of walking a mile in another person's shoes in order to understand how they experience and think about life.

Another instance of how BorderLinks has sought to begin with the perspective of the oppressed, letting them do the teaching, came about when the organization acquired the Casa Misericordia in Nogales, Sonora. It had been a retreat house for the Catholic Church for many years and offered some programs for families and their children in the surrounding area. Some may have thought that here was a perfect opportunity for folks from the privileged class and culture to take over what appeared to be a rather poorly run operation and fix it up for the poor Mexicans. Indeed, there were many US citizens more than willing to contribute to this project so that the Casa Misericordia could be "more effective" in its mission to the "disadvantaged."

But the founder, and then director, Rick Ufford-Chase, insisted on a different posture and course of action. The first thing that had to be done was to establish a few guidelines as to how and when any changes would be made in the programs and facilities of the Casa, and especially by whom. The Casa had been feeding lunch to over two hundred school children everyday on their way to or from school for over ten years with no help from any Anglos. In addition, clothes had been distributed and weekly mass had been held in the small chapel on a regular basis. The place had belonged to the surrounding Mexican community and they were in the best position to ascertain what changes were needed and how they could best be made.

Over the ensuing years many changes have indeed been made to the physical plant and to the programs offered by the Casa, all of which have developed and implemented by the bi-national staff and Board of Directors. The Casa has its own Mexican director who works in conjunction with the American director to facilitate the trips and programs aimed at educating North American visitors to the border. In addition, the Casa now serves as a fully functioning community center for the surrounding *colonias*, complete with a daycare facility. In addition, over the years several on site programs and opportunities have been developed, such as a co-operative market, a tree planting project, and instruction in sustainable technologies like simple solar ovens and composting toilets.

Some of these undertakings have ceased to remain operative simply because the persons who started them found it necessary to move away or take another job. In their place other projects and programs have sprung up, all of which underscores the indigenous and transient character of life on the border. In any case, the focus is always on what the current members of the communities want.

Yet a third instance which illustrates how BorderLinks tries to learn from the oppressed people on the border is the Semester on the Border program. In this program, about ten college students from a dozen schools around the country spend fifteen weeks living and studying on the border, dividing their stay between the Tucson, Arizona and Casa Misericordia campuses. In addition to five regular college courses, in which they read and discuss crucial border issues, these students participate in two travel seminars along the border and spend four weeks in homestays with border families.

Along with the homestays the semester students visit a number of Mexican sites and field placements where they learn from Mexican agencies and individuals about life on the other side of the border in a first-hand manner. Such opportunities include visits to immigration agencies, schools, and to local individuals such as artists and catholic sisters and priests working in parishes. It should also be mentioned that two or three of the teaching faculty for this semester program are themselves Mexican. In addition, there are several Mexican adjunct teachers who work with the students during their time south of the border. These opportunities are enriched by the two travel seminars that are an integral part of the semester program. It is truly an immersion experience.

The students in the semester program uniformly testify to the transformative experience this program provides for them. Paramount in their stories are their encounters with local people, including and especially children, with whom they have bonded and from whom they have learned a great deal, not only about the border, oppressions, and poverty, but about life in general. As one student put it: "My life and my values will never be the same. It will be difficult to return to my own family and community and not see them through very different eyes." Another said: "As a result of this semester I shower less, shop less, and have changed my major to mass communications because I feel I have a lot to say about life, the world, and my country."

Another activity in which semester students and other BorderLinks visitors alike participate is The Market Basket Survey. A simulated shopping trip to a Mexican super market goes a long way in the educational process because it makes one painfully aware of specific aspects of the border economy, some of which reinforce certain presuppositions while others upset them. Armed with a typical shopping list each partner works his or her way through the store noting down the prices of different basic foods. It is quite surprising to learn that the cost of food on the south side of the border is not much less than on the north side of the border. When this fact is coupled with the reality that the typical income on the south side of the border is around $200 or $300 per month it becomes obvious that it takes two people working at least full-time just to keep a family above the survival line.

Another surprise awaits those who shop on the border for food lies in the irony that many basic food stuffs, meat, milk, and eggs are less expensive on the north side. Thus many Mexican folks who can afford a daily border crossing permit regularly shop on the US side for these staples. This anomaly is explained by the high cost of transporting these items from central Mexico to the border region. An additional ironic twist to this situation is that because the people on border do much of their shopping in the US, a good deal of the income they earn in Mexico actually ends up in the coffers of American businesses. The Market Basket Survey is a big-time eye-opener for most North Americans.

2. The Fear of Freedom?

The paradox about who actually educates whom when it comes to border pedagogy is not the only surprising issue that confronts one in the exploration of the realities with which those on the Mexican side must live and work. Freire himself introduces the idea that oppressed people themselves have a deep-seated fear of the very freedom for which they seem to yearn. Because they have so internalized the values and concepts making up the oppressive world where they have lived for centuries, the idea of having to think and live outside of these categories is often very frightening. Freire puts it this way:

"One of the basic elements of the relationship between oppressor and oppressed is *prescription*. Every prescription represents the imposition of one person's choices upon another, transforming the consciousness of the person prescribed to into one that conforms with the prescriber's consciousness. Thus the behavior of the oppressed is prescribed behavior, following as it does the guidelines of the oppressor."[4]

Freire goes on to spell out the psychological damage of this paradoxical fear of freedom that lies deep within the consciousness of oppressed

4. Freire, *Pedagogy*, 46.

people in the following way: "The conflict lies in the choices between being wholly themselves or being divided: between ejecting the oppressor within or not ejecting them; between human solidarity or alienation . . . between acting or having the illusion of acting through the action of the oppressors. Between speaking out or being silent . . . This is the tragic dilemma of the oppressed which their education must take into account."[5]

It would be difficult if not impossible to contend that there is an equivalent paradoxical fear of freedom on the part of those of us in the oppressor class. For we have not been forced to live within and thus internalize a worldview conceived and implemented by someone other than ourselves. There is, however, a sense in which those of us in the oppressor class confront a dilemma of our own, namely that between maintaining our privileged position at the top of the socio-political and economic order while at the same time continuing to believe that our way of life embodies the high-level values of egalitarian democracy and religious or even non-religious humanism.

It is almost invariably the case that those countries, such as those in North America, which engage in economic exploitation and oppression of underdeveloped countries simultaneously maintain that they are the champions of freedom and justice which all others nations should emulate. Specifically at the economic level, North American nations clearly equate freedom, liberty, and the pursuit of happiness with the free enterprise economic system and open market capitalism. Thus it is generally concluded that those countries at the bottom of the world's economic order simply have not yet learned how to play the game, or are, "underdeveloped."

The result of this equating of economic and humanistic or religious values is a systemic denial of the possibility that the capitalistic free enterprise system can in any way be responsible for the horrendous difficulties faced by people in the developing countries of the world. It is this denial that creates the dilemma for a pedagogy of the oppressor which parallels the fear of freedom found in oppressed peoples of which Freire speaks. Thus it is that we in the US, as the primary exponents of the free enterprise system, are unable to see that we are also the primary cause of the poverty found among the developing countries. We cannot understand that poverty is not the natural result of laziness, inferior moral character, or lack of intelligence. Since we believe so strongly in the Great American Dream that anyone can, if they try hard, succeed, we are blinded to the fact that poverty

---

5. Freire, *Pedagogy*, 48.

never occurs naturally. It is, rather, often caused by certain historical events and economic policies which we as oppressors have put in motion.

What those of us in North America have consistently failed to realize, or rather, have consistently failed to admit to, is that there is a fundamental contradiction at the very heart of our understanding of the so-called free enterprise system. For it is common knowledge that in an open, competitive system there must inevitably exist a class of people who are at the bottom of the economic ladder upon whose cheap labor those at the top of the ladder depend for their profit margin.

Contrary to the great American belief that everyone can be a winner, in order for there to be a winner, there must be a large group of people who are by the very fact losers. In a competitive market a smart business person must do whatever he or she can to sell their product for the highest possible price while keeping costs, especially wages, at the lowest possible level. On the global scale this ideology often results in some countries being at the top of the system through oppressive exploitation.

This is why imperialist nations, whether in Europe from the sixteenth century through the nineteenth, or in North America in the twentieth and the twenty first centuries, have systematically sought to make use of technologically less developed countries throughout the world as their colonial labor base. In recent decades we in North America have packaged this economic dynamic in terms of the economic development of these less developed countries, especially those in Latin America, including Mexico. The fact remains, however, that the result is still exploitation. In the name of development we in the Western countries have defined those countries whose resources we want for our own developing technology and economy as *under*developed or as develop*ing* nations.

In Central America, as well as in several South American countries, this practice has resulted in entire national economies being devoted to producing one or two products, such as rubber, coffee, or sugar, for North American consumption. Thus the vast majority of people in these countries are unable to grow their own food, due to lack of space and/or time, and must then import food from other countries, especially the US, at higher prices.

This exploitation is demonstrated by the simple fact that whenever the cheap labor provided by the people of these less developed countries is in danger, for one reason or another, of drying up, the North American companies involved in producing and marketing these products relocate their operation to a place where the labor is cheaper. Moreover, these companies rarely provide any the benefits, such as health and pension funds, required by law in their own countries. It is clearly a case of oppression when the people of these poorer countries are exploited in this manner.

It must be acknowledged that a central role is played in this oppressive exploitation as well by the ruling upper class of every developing country under discussion here. The political and economic leaders controlling these countries are frequently themselves corrupt and co-operate with their North American investors to keep the system working, since they too profit by it. Mexico's political history speaks directly to this issue, as does the fact that it ranks fourth in the world in billionaires, right after the US, Germany, and Switzerland, with twenty eight. Yet Mexico remains one of the poorest nations in the world. Of course the majority of these billionaires do not live in Mexico and most of their money is in Swiss banks. It has not helped matters that until recently the same political party has remained in power for over seventy years.

The role played by the local politicians and aristocracy like Mexico in no way compares to or excuses the exploitative role played by North American so-called "multinational" companies. The quotation marks in the previous sentence are meant to call attention to the fact that such companies are anything but multinational since they in no way cooperate with the people of other nations in anything like a balanced fashion. Moreover, this exploitative role is in direct contradiction to the belief system and rhetoric of America's vowed ideology and commitment to free enterprise, democracy, and human rights.

What makes this whole scenario especially difficult is the fact that the US/Mexican border policy has been put in place precisely to keep this exploitive system functioning. While North American countries are free to locate their plants on the Mexican side of the border, with little or no commitment to the Mexican government or the workers, and to transport their finished products back to North America tax free, it remains the case that Mexican workers are not free to move across the border into the US seeking better paying jobs. The North American Free Trade Agreement is not set up to benefit Mexican workers in any way. When workers are basically bound to one geographic area, free enterprise does not exist.

There are many political thinkers and activists who have been trying to point out these fundamental contradictions in this neo-liberal or global economy for some time now. One thinker who is particularly helpful is

George Soros. Soros is well-known as a major player in world capitalism and philanthropy. Although he continues to make a great deal of money and to share it with worthy causes, Soros has become critical of North American capitalism because it operates without humanistic values and social concern for those it claims to benefit. He argues cogently that an economic system should be meant to serve people rather than the other way around, and capitalism as we know it fails to do this. There no longer is an invisible hand, to use Adam Smith's famous phrase that guides economic operations towards the long range common good.   Soros contends that capitalism must always be regulated carefully so as to bring about the good life for all the people concerned. Thus the hand that guides the economic process must be as visible and intentional as possible so that the common good of all levels of society can be maximized. Behind this approach lies the basic assumption that human beings exist socially prior to existing in-dividually, a belief that runs contrary to the rank individualism which has come to characterize modern society, especially in North America.

This then is the paradox that confronts those of us who live in the richest nation in the history of the world. While we claim to believe in and support the freedom and well-being of all people, the economic system by which we live and prosper disproportionately belies these values. The problem, then, for a pedagogy of the oppressor is to discover ways to raise our consciousness concerning this basic contradiction. In some ways this contradiction parallels that of the fear of freedom which Freire finds among oppressed peoples, because it by and large goes entirely unnoticed and is difficult to surface amidst the psychological and cultural pressures bom-barding them. The people of the oppressed countries have an unarticulated fear of being set free from their oppressive context, while those of us in oppressor countries have an unarticulated fear of admitting that our way of life is actually self-contradictory at its base.

The pedagogical challenge with respect to this fear of freedom syn-drome that resides within many if not most people in oppressed societies is to help them come to understand the factors that create this situation, as well as their own potential for doing something about it. Likewise, the pedagogical challenge with respect to the fundamental contradiction lying at the base of the ideology believed in by those of us doing the oppressing is to help us admit that we are not even close to where we think we are, and to motivate ourselves to do something to free us from it.

When the BorderLinks organization confronts the dilemma inherent within the foregoing paradox, it must do so with a great deal of circumspection. For it is not only contrary to the BorderLinks vision to play on North American peoples' guilt, but it would in the long run prove to be a counterproductive strategy. Guilt may well motivate people to salve their conscience with paternalistic charity, but it will do little or nothing to change the overall value system of the persons involved. Consciousness is not raised by direct methods of instruction and/or indoctrination.

When a person or group signs on to do a BorderLinks trip they are sent a reading packet to be read prior to their arrival in Tucson, AZ. This packet has reprinted articles and news items that explain the particular realities faced by those folks living on the border, especially along the Mexican side. This packet is continuously being revised in order to assure that the information is up to date. It constitutes an initial effort to allow the learner to come into contact with the realities of the border on his or her own.

Upon arrival the delegates are given several orientation sessions in order for them to get to know one another and the BorderLinks staff in charge of their trip, as well as to discuss various items in the reading packet. A crucial part of these orientation sessions is an articulation and sharing of the participants' hopes, fears, and questions about the adventure upon which they are about to embark. Many folks express concerns about safety and health, while at the same time hoping that they will learn a great deal about the border reality, as well as about themselves.

Here again it is important to recall that consciousness raising is a subtle process because one is dealing with a holistic mindset rather than simply with a matter of information transfer. Often when individuals ask questions of the trip leaders, the most appropriate response is simply: "Why not wait and see what you yourself experience about that issue during our time in Mexico." Actually interacting with a given reality, and especially with the people who live it, is the best and perhaps the only way to restructure a person's paradigm or model of a given reality.

Throughout any BorderLinks travel experience along the border, the emphasis is continually on providing North Americans experiences to see for themselves how people do in fact live. Hopefully, this direct encounter will trigger questions about why it is like it is and what might be done about it. Homestays, interviews, shopping trips, as well as visits to *maquiladoras* and the Border Patrol are all aimed at immersing those of us of the privileged class in the everyday life of those living the border reality.

As Freire points out, whenever one is confronted with the possibility of a reality that is beyond or other than what is familiar, it is natural to seek various defenses in order to be able to avoid actually dealing with this fresh possibility. BorderLinks is quite familiar with the invention of such devices which we North Americans use to shift responsibility for the conditions on the border to someone else. As is well known, it is quite useless to try to deal with defense mechanisms by direct confrontation, because the defenses just entrench themselves ever more deeply.

It must be admitted that this is perhaps the most difficult feature of the entire BorderLinks pedagogical process. It is always tempting and far easier to simply explain straight off how and why it is that things are as they are, who is to blame and what we North Americans need to do about it. Once one has come to an understanding of the issues involved and has formulated conclusions about them, much in the same way they have been outlined on the previous pages, then it becomes very hard not to expound on these points in a very direct manner. A better approach, and the one that BorderLinks is committed to, is to arrange the introduction to the US/Mexico border in an experiential way so that there is no occasion for us North Americans to engage in defensive maneuvers. When there is no confrontation involved, it is much easier for a person to assimilate information and experiences so as to be able to deal with them appropriately.

I well remember the first time I really read the sign at the border which announces that no firearms are allowed in Mexico. No one had ever pointed this sign out to me and when I actually grasped what it means in relation to the entire debate about gun control in the US, especially in light of all the recent killings of children in our schools, the significance of this sign really hit me deeply. A lecture on the subject of gun control would not have been half as powerful.

Among the usual sorts of defense maneuvers that we North Americans engage in, has to do with falling back on traditional stereotypes about people of developing countries in general and perhaps Mexican people in particular. Probably everyone knows of the stereotype that they are basically lazy and probably intellectually inferior. At least their culture is more laid back and less industrious than most of Europe and America. This is why, it is often claimed, they are so happy yet economically and technologically behind.

There once was a cartoon in the New Yorker magazine that depicted a native chief and a foreigner sitting on the porch of the chief's hut. The chief said: "Frankly I've never thought of our culture as underdeveloped. I've always thought of your culture as overdeveloped." It is not difficult to argue that North America has worked its way into an industrial and technological bind from which there seems to be no escape. Our entire nation is held hostage to our unrelenting commitment to convenience and comfort. We will never have enough energy to power all the gadgets and devices we will continue to invent and demand, and huge brown-outs continue to deprive entire regions of electricity for days at a time. Our motto really is: "The one who dies with the most toys wins." And stress is our favorite merit badge. Indeed, the concept of being over developed strikes us as totally meaningless.

The fact of the matter is, the people of Mexico are every bit as hard working as we are, as anyone who witnesses many of them working two jobs can clearly see. Moreover, their society is one that still values family and cultural life more highly than most post industrialized societies. It is only in recent decades that, having been drawn into our own economic process, Mexican culture has begun to implode on itself. Nevertheless, anyone who has observed, or hired, Mexican workers in the US knows full well that they are extremely hard working and loyal.

The other common defense mechanism is to say that at least these Mexican people on the border have jobs. If it were not for the US *maquiladoras*, it is sometimes claimed, the Mexican people would be starving to death. In this sense, it is often claimed, the system does work, for even the people who are at the bottom of the scale are better off than they would have been without these jobs. Although the wages are low, about one dollar an hour, they are about double Mexico's national minimum standard wage.

In a sense this line of defense seems to hold water, but it fails to deal with the fact that there is no job security in this industry, nor are there any health and pension benefits beyond the minimal ones provided by the Mexican government. In addition, this way of thinking stops short of dealing with the question of why all these people are flocking to the border, and beyond, seeking asylum and work. The simple fact is that the Mexican government's commitment to economic privatization, at the behest of the US government, has so stimulated the American agro-business industry in central Mexico that there is no longer any future for family farming in this region. The assembly plant jobs are all that exist.

One way BorderLinks seeks to educate its participants about such economic realities is by taking them to visit some *maquiladoras*. Here they can ask questions of the manager or public relations person who guides their tour. Questions about job turnover rates, employee regulations, safety standards, and company investments, or lack thereof, are frequently raised. In this way the dilemmas involved in the contradictions inherent within border capitalism get addressed, albeit indirectly. The hope is that these answers, together with the obvious facts of the border reality will serve to erode the rationalizations implicit within the mindset of the oppressors.

This whole scenario of the border economy has demanded a huge removal of people from their farmlands, and rendered them to the border region, not to mention to the US itself seeking asylum. People have often been forced to leave their families and homes when they migrate to the border, resulting in great confusion as well as pain and sorrow. When they arrive in a border town they are crowded into tiny houses in neighborhoods where they know almost no one and where there are almost no public services, such as water, electricity, and sewage disposal. It is no wonder that the suicide and depression rates among such displaced persons are very high.

In short, although there are some extenuating circumstances that contribute to the horrific conditions along the border, by far the major cause of the despair, poverty, and disease is the oppressive economic reality, most of which is the result of North American capitalistic endeavors. Here again, it needs to be stressed that piling up guilt on folks who have come to see the US/Mexican border reality serves little purpose. Rather it is to raise consciousness that groups like BorderLinks exist for. Whenever consciousness is raised, it is possible that consciences are also raised.

3. Reversed Oppression?

Another paradox addressed in Freire's work is that of the perennial problem facing those who actually do effect a near total transformation of their oppressive situation. Do they turn around and oppress those who had oppressed them? Is reversed oppression inevitable? The exact nature of any post-revolutionary period has always been problematic because it is never quite clear how the oppressors and the oppressed are to relate to one another during and after socio-political transformation. There have been instances in recent history where a serious effort, and sometimes with noteworthy success, has been made to avoid the pattern of reversing oppression after a transformation. Nelson Mandela and his colleagues working in South Africa after the fall of Apartheid was a stellar example.

This challenge is similar to those that have arisen in the US around racism, on the one hand and feminism, on the other. The institution of affirmative action policies and the efforts to pass an Equal Rights Amendment and other, more recent social action efforts caused a great deal of debate about the fairness of such efforts to level the playing field. Racial and gender oppression are generally agreed to be wrong, and need of correction. But it is difficult to get agreement on how such inequities should be dealt with. Are those who were last in line now to be put first in line? Here, too, we hear accusations of reverse racism and token feminism, and the like.

Freire speaks to this issue quite directly when he insists that the entire dynamic of oppression, for both the oppressor and the oppressed, is a dehumanizing one. He then argues that: "Because it is a distortion of being more fully human, sooner or later being less human leads the oppressed to struggle against those who made them so. In order for this struggle to have meaning, the oppressed must not, in seeking to regain their humanity . . . become in turn oppressors of the oppressors, but rather restorers of humanity to both."[6]

Nevertheless, Freire acknowledges that far too often it is the case, especially in the early stages of a revolution, that the uprising oppressed seek in turn to oppress those by whom they themselves were oppressed. They do this because they have absorbed their vision of what true humanity is from their oppressors. Thus they simply recapitulate the behavior of their oppressors in seeking to rectify their situation. It is, in Freire's view, the modern European/American philosophy of individualism that contributes strongly to this model of continuing dehumanization. When a people lose hold on the social fabric of their shared existence, whether as an oppressor or as the oppressed, they lose the ability to think in terms of the common good.

One of the most penetrating analyses of this reversed oppression dynamic is offered by Franz Fanon in his well-known book *The Wretched of the Earth*. In his chapter "The Pitfalls of National Consciousness" Fanon outlines the dangers besetting those who would seek to overthrow their oppressors in the name of nationalism. Of particular concern is the temptation of those people who were the middle men in a colonized situation, in between the imperialist oppressors and the oppressed, to simply repeat the oppressive pattern instituted by the ruling class once they have been

---

6. Freire, *Pedagogy*, 44.

deposed. We have witnessed this dynamic throughout the countries that became independent after the Second World War, especially in Africa.

In essence, the same colonial hierarchy remains in place with different people taking over the roles of the ruling class. Even though, or perhaps because, these new rulers are generally indigenous people themselves, they refuse to see their revolution as an opportunity to truly liberate their country. Instead they fall into fulfilling the very roles and traps that they accused their colonial rulers of instituting. As Freire says, they have so internalized the individualist values of their imperialist oppressors that they are blind to any other way of existing and leading. "Their vision of the new man or woman is individualistic; because of their identification with the oppressor, they have no consciousness of themselves as persons or as members of an oppressed class."[7]

Fanon was very upset by the tendency of those who have replaced their colonial oppressors to completely overlook the needs and wants of the more oppressed class in the name of the National Consciousness. Only those dwelling in cities and those engaged in commerce receive attention and assistance. In this way everything remains the same even though it is often claimed that liberation has taken place. In reality, things are actually worse, since the ruling class is now entirely made up of native peoples themselves. The oppressed are now the oppressors.

In describing the transformational process Freire insist that only the oppressed can liberate both themselves and their oppressors because they alone experience and thus understand the dehumanizing character of the oppressive hierarchy. Out of their struggle for liberation will emerge a new humanity that will transcend both the oppressor class and the oppressed class. "If the goal of the oppressed is to become fully human, they will not achieve their goal by simply changing poles ... the moment the new regime hardens into a dominating 'bureaucracy' the humanist dimension of the struggle is lost."[8]

Freire goes on to argue that once the ruling class has been set aside there will need to be policies for maintaining a truly humanitarian society. This will mean that those who were oppressors will feel that they are being discriminated against because they will no longer enjoy the special privileges they once did. The theoretic and/or religious basis for their posture of

7. Freire, *Pedagogy*, 46.

8. Freire, *Pedagogy*, 56–57.

enlightenment will have been removed and they will naturally experience this as reversed oppression. Here is how Freire puts it:

> Resolution of the oppressor-oppressed contradiction indeed implies the disappearance of the oppressors as the dominant class. However, the restraints imposed by the former oppressed on their oppressors, so that the latter cannot resume their former position, do not constitute oppression. An act is oppressive only when it prevents people from being more fully human . . . Acts which prevent the restoration of the formerly oppressive class cannot be compared with those which create and maintain it, cannot be compared with those by which a few people deny the majority their right to be human. [9]

Yet another aspect of this whole dilemma of the possibility of reversed oppression is focused in the potential for and justification of violence on the part of the oppressed as they struggle for their own and their oppressors' liberation. The tack Freire takes here is to suggest a broader understanding of the notion of violence itself. His point is that those who have suffered under systematic oppression cannot help having internalized the violent and oppressive values of their oppressors. Thus there will be a certain duality in their own value system which may express itself in the way they go about their struggle.

"Any situation in which 'A' objectively exploits 'B' or hinders his or her pursuit of self-affirmation as a responsible person is one of oppression. Such a situation itself constitutes violence, even when sweetened by false generosity, because it interferes with the person's ontological and historical vocation to be more fully human. With the establishment of an oppressive situation, violence has already begun . . . Violence initiated by those who oppress, who exploit, who fail to recognize others as persons—not by those who have been oppressed, exploited, and unrecognized."[10]

Moreover, Freire contends, any violent acts engaged in by the oppressed class seeking full human liberation have as their goal the overthrow of the oppressive hierarchical system and are thus actually justified or at least necessary. In fact, it is possible to see such violence as an act of love if it aims at the ultimate wellbeing of all humans, including the oppressor class. Perhaps the term 'discipline' might better express this claim, such as when a parent disciplines a child, or a society disciplines criminals in order to help them

9. Freire, *Pedagogy*, 56–57.
10. Freire, *Pedagogy*, 55.

understand the wrongful nature of their hurtful behavior. The use of force is not always violent, and can in fact be used wisely and even redemptively.

As Freire says: "Whereas the violence of the oppressors prevents the oppressed from being fully human, the response of the latter to this violence is grounded in the desire to pursue the right to be human. As the oppressors dehumanize others and violate their rights, they themselves also become dehumanized. As the oppressed, fighting to be human, take away the oppressors' power to dominate and suppress, they restore to the oppressors the humanity they had lost in the exercise of oppression."[11]

Perhaps one way to interpret Freire's view here is in terms of the notion of the preferential option for the poor that plays such a crucial role in the movement known as Liberation Theology generated by the work of such thinkers as Gustavo Gutierrez. The logic here would be that since God's love and grace are meant to be shed on all people, those who are being denied these gifts by others must be given preference because at this point in history they are being left out of God's overall plan. This may look like reverse discrimination but in point of fact it is not, because any situation from which God's love and grace are being excluded must be overturned. In the same way, if the justice on which a society is based is not reaching those at the bottom of the society, then something must be done to radically restructure the society.

There are, to be sure, other ways to effect socio-political liberation than violent revolution. Even Karl Marx suggested that it might be achieved through democratic processes, and we have seen this happen in the liberation of the black people of South Africa and various instances of the establishment of democratic rule in different countries around the world, perhaps especially in the United States itself. Indeed, even in bringing our own Civil War to an end, President Lincoln effected the reuniting of the American people without punishing the southern states.

In many ways, to be sure, all this talk about violence and post-revolutionary polices is not directly relevant to the pedagogy of the oppressed as practiced by BorderLinks. Nevertheless, it is useful to explore the sorts of solutions and transformations that may be suggested by North Americans who come to visit the border, and what sort of responses to these proposals might be given by those folks living along the border. In addition, it may be well to consider some of the actual dynamics that

11. Freire, *Pedagogy*, 56.

take place between the North Americans who live at the border and those Mexicans who live and work there.

It must be said at the outset that in spite of the huge amount and extreme degree of violence perpetrated upon the people of Mexico over the past five hundred years by the imperialist powers of Spain, Portugal, France, and the United States, the Mexican people are by and large not bitter nor angry. There is of course some tendency for the Mexican people to blame countries other than their own for their troubles and hardships, and there is clear historical reason for so doing. In the main, however, the people of Mexico remain open to North Americans, as well as to their own future.

One of the factors that has, nonetheless, contributed to the general malaise affecting a great many Mexicans is the inefficiency of their own electoral process. For over seventy years one political party, the PRI, was completely dominant throughout every branch of the Mexican government. However, the election of Vicente Fox and the PAN party to the Presidency in the year two thousand did much to empower the people to believe that they themselves can make a real difference in their own lives. Things have not, however, continued to develop positively in the ensuing years.

In the final analysis it has been the Mexican people's dependency on and nearness to the United States that lies at the heart of the difficulties for the Mexican people. As the saying goes: "Poor Mexico, so far from God and so close to the United States." As was mentioned earlier in this book, the US/Mexico border may well be the only place in the world where in one step a person can go from the so called first world to the third world. The strong contrast resulting from the nearness of, yet distance between, our two countries strongly contributes to the Mexican people's negative self-image.

A case in point may be found in BorderLinks' initial efforts to establish, with the help of a $25,000 grant administered by the University of Arizona, a microcredit banking opportunity for some women in Nogales, Sonora. At first it was very difficult to get the half dozen women chosen for the project to understand and believe that such a thing was possible and they themselves could be trusted to make it work. They were unfamiliar with dealing with money and they had very little confidence in their own ability to borrow, let alone pay back, even small sums of money. The convolutions of the dynamics involved in these processes were complex and at times painful, but over time these women gained confidence and experience from developing their tamale factory in one of the family homes.

At the international level, of course, a great deal needs to be done to rectify the unilateral dependency character of the relationship between the Mexican people and the United States. It is hardly realistic to expect North Americans to renounce their dominance of Mexico, but it might be possible to work out at more fair and symbiotic relationship which allows and even encourages Mexican workers to obtain temporary US work permits while requiring *maquiladoras* to pay a livable wage, even by Mexican standards. This latter tack would greatly reduce the need for border militarization and avoid hundreds of deaths yearly in the Sonoran Desert. A similar alternative approach to the current US asylum process would even help more.

In January 1994 the Zapatista movement, based in the work and teachings of Emiliano Zapata, one of the key leaders in the Mexican revolution, and led by one Subcomandante Marcos, made its entry into Mexican politics in response to the implementation to the NAFTA agreement. The Zapatistas announced that this treaty signaled the death notice for indigenous people because it established the priority of privatization over community autonomy in the Mexican economy. This meant the end of thousands of community farms, or *ejidos*, which eradicated the vast majority of peasant farming. The Zapatistas took charge of a number of cities in their Chiapas area for several days without in any way attempting to effect a military coup of the Mexican government. There was a minimum of bloodshed, but afterwards the Mexican president had the military hunt the Zapatistas down and imprisoned or killed many of them.

The whole catastrophe was followed by a series of peace talks with President Fox and the Mexican legislators. At first there was hope that a fair agreement could be reached, but eventually the talks broke down and things returned to pretty much normal. The role of community farms, which were the backbone of the Mexican people's livelihood, was essentially eradicated, and this is one reason that thousands of Mexican families were forced to move to the border to find work in the *maquiladoras*. Some have suggested that there was serious high level collusion at the heart of all these events involving the Mexican government and the US companies owning the *maquiladoras*.

Particularly interesting in light of Freire's discussion of the dynamics of reversed oppression and the role of violence in transformation, is the unusual mode of operation adopted by the Zapatistas. Although they had consistently portrayed themselves as a military force, at the same time they refused to engage in any form of aggression. Moreover, their leader,

Subcomandante Marcos produced a continuous flow of communiques in which he prodded and embarrassed the Mexican government through an assortment of shrewd political and economic analyses, poetry, and humorous diatribes.

Right from the outset the Zapatistas made it clear that they were not in the least interested in taking over the Mexican government. Rather, their stated aim was to stand as a witness against the oppression of the Mexican people, both in Chiapas and throughout the world, until the oppression was lifted. In all his communications Marcos insisted that indigenous people do not want to be left out of the modern world in order to return to the life they had known prior to imperialist colonization. Instead, they wanted to have a full say in determining their own destiny and a full share in what the future might hold for all the people of Mexico.

Thus it was a fortuitous occasion for the BorderLinks semester program to have some of its students actually attend the official welcoming of the Zapatistas to the Mexican capitol in connection with their History of Mexico class. In more recent months many of the current semester students have been able to participate in various rallies held in Tucson and the surrounding area on behalf of the efforts to legalize millions of undocumented immigrants now working in the US. Other groups visiting the border through BorderLinks also have had opportunities to observe various border coalitions working on behalf of border peoples and issues. These field trips, as they might be called, constitute a vital part of the BorderLinks educational program.

It is at this point that the Zapatista movement spoke directly to the concern about violence in socio-political transformation. As Freire insists, the true basis of any and all revolution is educational in nature. Pedagogy is the only authentic means of transformation. It is clear that the Zapatistas fully understood the educational value of their revolutionary activity from the outset and sought to remain true to it throughout the years of their sustained efforts to reform Mexican government and politics. In particular, they showed no interest in becoming the ruling class or of engaging in anything like reversed oppression.

As time went by the Zapatistas entirely redefined their role in relation to Mexican politics. They began to make videos about the situation of the indigenous people in Chiapas and Mexico at large in order to educate the rest of the world, along with the Mexican people, about the many injustices they encounter in their daily lives. Moreover, they presented themselves as a political party without actually entering into the official political arena.

All of the foregoing is directly relevant to the BorderLinks educational vision and programs because it is exactly by means of the key role of education that it seeks to identify itself and guide all of its endeavors. BorderLinks is committed to what Freire calls "the eminently pedagogical character of the revolution,"[12] and firmly believes that it is through the education of North Americans that significant change can be brought to the US/Mexico border. It is the dialogical nature of authentic pedagogy, to which we shall turn in the next chapter that guards against tendencies toward reversed oppression because dialogue is symbiotic rather than unilateral in character. True education seeks the full humanity of all persons, including the present oppressors.

Freire sums all this up in the following way: "The pedagogy of the oppressed, as a humanist and libertarian pedagogy has two distinct stages. In the first, the oppressed unveil the world of oppression and through this praxis commit themselves to its transformation. In the second stage . . . this pedagogy ceases to belong to the oppressed and becomes a pedagogy of all the people in the process of permanent liberation."[13]

4. Liberating the Oppressor?

Perhaps the most ironic paradox of oppression revolves around the idea that those who stand in the greatest need of liberation are the oppressors themselves. The most obvious form of oppression is that perpetrated onto the poor and exploited class by the ruling class. In reality, according to Freire, this sort of oppression is but a symptom of a much deeper oppression, namely that by which the ruling class itself is held captive. There are at least three main levels or dimensions of this oppression from which oppressors themselves need liberation.

The first of these pertains to the ruling class's addiction to a materialistic value system. For decades it has been popular in western culture to criticize communist countries for their "Godless materialism" because the theory behind it is called dialectical materialism. Aside from the fact that this criticism is based on a basic misunderstanding of what Karl Marx meant by the term materialism, it should be quite clear to anyone who

12. Freire, *Pedagogy*, 67.

13. Freire, *Pedagogy*, 54.

bothers to look that North American society is probably the most materialistic society that has ever existed.

We are, in fact, fundamentally addicted to the consumption and acquisition of material goods, such as cars and technological gadgets, as well
as to the compulsion to earn or win a lot of money, either by swinging a
big business deal or by getting lucky at the casino, racetrack, or lottery.
John Kenneth Galbraith had it right in the title of his book, *The Acquisitive
Society*. So did the bumper stickers that carry our slogans: "The one who
dies with the most toys wins." And: "Shop 'til I drop."

One of the more insidious manifestations of this materialism is the
endless yet almost unnoticed encroachment of the world of commerce into
every aspect of North American culture. Corporate sponsorship and even-
tual control of nearly all dimensions of society has become a matter of fact
pattern. Everything from education and art to sports and religion, not to
mention holidays and politics, has been co-opted by commercial enterprise.
Nearly all major sports events are named after or owned by businesses, and
even schools and colleges are beholden to those corporations who sponsor
their lunch and athletic programs.

What is truly amazing about this phenomenon is that by and large
this materialistic trend is not only permitted but is either defended in the
name of free enterprise or goes completely unnoticed. Nothing is thought
of the fact that the evening news broadcasts are sponsored by big name
products, although thirty years ago this was not the case and still is not
the case in most European countries. Freedom of the press and free enterprise are not good bedfellows, for there is a subtle connection between
sponsorship and control that is difficult to alter once the proverbial camel
has its nose inside the tent.

Hand in hand with the addiction to acquisition goes the commitment
to possession. The desire to own material objects has itself become an obsession in North American society, and this obsession in turn leads to the need
to control people as well as things. "This is mine, you can't have it," becomes
the motto of cultures that develop an aristocracy based on money, as Alexis
de Tocqueville said it would in his profound book *Democracy in America*.

Freire addresses this connection between ownership and possession
in the following manner: "In their unrestrained eagerness to possess, the
oppressors develop the conviction that it is possible for them to transform
everything into objects of their purchasing power, hence their strictly
materialistic concept of existence. Money is the measure of all things, and

profit the primary goal. For the oppressors what is worthwhile is to have more—always more, even at the cost of the oppressed having less or having nothing. For them, *to be is to have* and to be the class of the 'haves.'"[14]

A second dimension of the oppression from which oppressors need liberating is that of racism. Although Freire never addresses this topic directly, it is clearly in the background of nearly all he has to say about the oppressor class. For there can be no mistake, and it is surely no accident, that the line between the so called First and Second and especially the Third worlds is drawn according to color and race. The people of Latin America, along with those of India, Africa, and Asia have always been and still are viewed as vastly inferior by those of us living in Europe and the US.

By and large those of us who are white have continuously tried to conquer, control, and exploit people who are not because we are convinced that we are superior to them. Not only have Americans, along with Europeans, enslaved people of color, but we have attempted to annihilate those people who were living in North America when Europeans arrived on the scene and claimed to have discovered this continent. This racist dynamic comprises a large part of the oppression about which Freire writes and against which he contends.

The story of the role racism played in the invasion of the Americas by the *conquistadores* is well known. Initially the invaders did not even acknowledge that the indigenous peoples were human beings. If not for the insistence of a few people, such as Bartolome de Las Casas, it is not clear whether this would have ever changed. Even after the pope ruled that native people have souls, they were continually dehumanized and exploited. In essence, of course, nothing was ever really done about changing the policies and practices that enslaved an entire continent. It is said that de Las Casas was assured that the powers in charge of things in Europe "would look into these matters."

One of the deep ironies in the history of Latin America is that while in modern times all countries have come to honor the greatness of the ancient indigenous civilizations, such as the Mayans, they continue to treat contemporary native peoples oppressively. This is parallel to the way North Americans romantically extol the virtues of Native Americans after nearly annihilating them a little over a hundred years ago. Even today American Indians remain oppressed within our own society, even as we extol them by naming automobiles after them and collect their artifacts as art treasures.

14. Freire, *Pedagogy*, 58.

Mexican society has always suffered from the racism of those that pretend that their own heritage is directly tied to Spain. Even those who clearly drive from a mixed heritage oppress those who are purely "Indian." On the US/Mexico border it is the racism embodied in the Anglo culture that dominates Mexican peoples. Participants in BorderLinks trips along the border not only see this racism, but they experience it when they return home. One young man was brought to tears by the way his own family spoke about the migrant workers in his home town. He said to them: "You are talking about the sort of people I have been living with. They are wonderful people; warm, loving, and friendly. They work hard in order to support their families."

The third dimension from which the oppressive class needs liberating lies at an even deeper level, for it pertains to the basic individualism that undergirds the very worldview within and by which western civilization lives. At the base of western culture, beginning at least with the classical Greek society, rests the assumption that people exist as essentially self-contained individual atoms that can choose whether or not to enter into various social relationships and associations as they wish in the name of freedom and or rugged individualism. This atomism lies behind all that North Americans hold true and dear.

This individualist view of human nature and approach to social reality received a great deal of reinforcement in modern times with the overthrow of European monarchies and the rise of democracy. It also grew along with the efforts to liberate people from the dominance of the Roman Catholic Church which had held sway all though the Middle Ages. Although it is difficult to gainsay the virtues of the democratic ideology in the struggle for freedom from the tyranny of authoritarian domination, this view of human nature and social reality is not without serious problems.

From a strictly logical point of view, for instance, it must be admitted that social groups, such as bands, tribes, and families must be seen as more fundamental than individuals, since the latter can only come into existence within the former. Individuals, as such, arise within the context and dynamics of groups, not the other way around, and thus there exist values which are more basic and important than the rights and freedoms of individuals. The latter are secondary or parasitic on prior existing social values. First came and come the cooperative values of family, community, and the common good. There are no individuals, as such, apart from some form of social reality.

As long as people think of themselves as essentially independent units which are free to pursue self-fulfillment in their own way and time, there will be destructive competition and oppression. This was the political issue involved in the Civil War between the states. Are individual states more basic than the union of the states, and thus free to project their own laws above those of the nation as a whole? Or, do not the needs and concerns of the country as a whole take precedence over those of the individual states? This is also the key issue confronting our world today. It is beginning to look as though the very notion of individual nation states needs to be re-thought altogether if we are to survive on this planet. That is the reason for the United Nations organization.

In his critique of the way in which the oppressed class internalizes the values of the oppressor class so that they are unable to see themselves as free and capable persons, Freire traces this inability to the individualistic values of the oppressor class. He argues that since the only worldview available to the oppressed is one in which some individuals rule over others, the oppressed also desire to become full persons who can live and control others as free individuals. Speaking of the oppressed person's self-image, Freire says: "The vision of the new man or woman is individualistic. Because of their identification with the oppressor, they have no consciousness of themselves as persons or as members of an oppressed class . . . It is the rare peasant who, once 'promoted' to overseer does not become more of a tyrant towards his former comrades than the owner himself. This is because of the context of the peasant's situation that is oppression, remains unchanged."[15]

Now the crucial point to keep in mind here is that the foregoing analysis of the three dimensions of the oppression, materialism, racism, and individualism, from which the oppressor class needs to be liberated is not offered as a critique of the oppressor class as such. Rather it is presented in order to make the point that in ways perhaps less obvious but more pernicious, the oppressor class too is held captive by its own worldview and value system. The very characteristics listed above themselves constitute a mode of bondage for those living in the privileged class, a bondage from which they need liberating if they too are to be fully human.

In Freire's analysis, of course, this liberation of the oppressor class must originate with those who are oppressed thereby if both classes of people are to achieve liberation and full humanness. This is why he himself was dedicated to the education of the oppressed, since the transformation of the

15. Freire, *Pedagogy*, 46.

world must begin with and come from those who are disenfranchised. The oppressor class will never effect such a transformation on its own initiative, since it will never willingly give up its domination of the socio-political and economic processes. Moreover, it is at present unable to see and/or admit that its own worldview and value system is itself a form of oppression.

It remains true, however, that the oppressor class can and must also be transformed, albeit in a more indirect and subtle manner. Given this understanding of the total situation, it remains very difficult for an enterprise such as BorderLinks to know how to go about the pedagogy of the oppressor. It will hardly do to approach the oppressor head-on by pointing out that his or her value system and worldview themselves function as a form of oppression for those who live according to them. Once again, the key to this situation lies in the indirect rather than direct interaction with those one is seeking to educate. Moreover, this indirect methodology must be grounded in the realities of the lives of those who live as the oppressed.

Perhaps the most obvious strategy is simply that of taking North Americans to the US/Mexico border and arranging for them to interact with and get to know the folks who live there. As nearly everyone knows, there is something almost magical about how our views of a person or situation change as a result of getting to know them more thoroughly. In addition, our own understanding of ourselves changes as well from such encounters. Walking in another person's shoes provides us with new experiences and a fresh angle of vision from which to see better the world around us.

This is why, of course, BorderLinks spends most of its time and energy finding ways to bring people from North America together with people on the border. The hope is that such face-to-face human interaction will not only enable North Americans to see the realities of the border existence, but will also enable them to gain a whole new perspective on their own lives and values. This process is the beginning of what might well lead to the liberation of some oppressors from the bondage in which they "live and move and have their being," but of which they are unaware.

The specifics of this methodology are those that have already been presented in the description of the BorderLinks programs earlier on. Arranging for North Americans to stay overnight and eat meals with Mexican families on the border, as well as setting up encounters and interviews with people and agencies that make up the context of border existence, all contribute to the possibility of seeing the realities of the border and one's own value system in a fresh light. In addition, having opportunity to read about and discuss these realties with BorderLinks staff and faculty can make a strong contribution to shaping this fresh perspective.

Here again, the primary concern is to create an arena where personal and social transformation can arise, without forcing certain ideas or points of view on anyone. This, of course, requires a great deal of trust in the people living on the border, as well as in the dynamics of the transformational process. The emphasis is on enabling North Americans to see and feel what is actually in front and all around them, and on helping them formulate and probe questions that arise naturally from what they see and feel. It is truly exciting and rewarding when a person makes a discovery in this process.

The results of this mode of education are not always seen right away. Frequently, however, people who have participated in a BorderLinks delegation will write or call later to share their gratitude for the opportunity and the radical character of their new understanding of themselves. This new understanding is often expressed in volunteering or even full-time service work with one of various activist and social organizations along the border. One other, and only one, indication of these transformations is the amazing continuous financial support BorderLinks continues to receive from its former participants.

One particular conversation among such participants gives an indication of the nature and depth of the sort of rebirth these experiences can give, along with some concrete ideas as to how it might express itself in one's daily life. In the midst of a discussion about the border realities, one person shared her dismay over the incomprehensible magnitude of the difficulties involved at the border. She pointed out that we are dealing here with world-wide patterns and individual selfishness, among many other things. This discouragement was shared by many of those present. One young fellow answered that the whole thing does not seem so impossible if one simply begins with one's own life. There are things one person can do, he said, and he began to describe how he has tried to change how he lives in small ways. He now tries to buy far fewer clothes, and to share the things he does own with others. Another person commented that he and his wife now have a rule that they will never buy new clothes without giving some to those in need. Yet another said that at their home they work hard at saving resources, recycling, not throwing away food, and not using or buying every new gadget on the market.

In a somewhat different vein, another person suggested that one can get involved with volunteer groups and political activists in order to try to change local and national policies with regard to economics, immigration, and the environment. Yet another person suggested that actually living and working with the poor and homeless would be a concrete way to establish solidarity with the oppressed.

To return to the main emphasis of our current section, all of the above suggestions, while in some cases actually helping the folks in the oppressed class, were aimed at liberating those participating in the discussion from their own oppression at the hands of the individualistic, materialistic, and racist Western worldview. The concern in the conversation was not so much about doing away with poverty, exploitation, and domination of the less privileged by the more privileged class. Rather it was about beginning to do away with the bondage that we in the privileged world, or more correctly, the over privileged class find ourselves immersed in.

At the close of yet a different discussion, the same young woman who had spent an entire semester living and studying on the border, referred to an earlier discussion in which she had put the whole thing quite bluntly when she said: "This has been the most important experience of my young life. I will never be able to look at the world the same way as I did before coming here. I definitely plan to get involved in some form of activism when I return home. And because of the way my family and community feel about such things, I know it's not going to be easy. But I am a new person after and because of this experience."

Hopefully this examination of the paradoxes that beset the concept and the practice of oppression, has at the very least set the stage for the explorations that are to follow. Freire's analysis of revolutionary pedagogy becomes far more specific in his ensuing chapters, and thus so must these reflections on his thought as it applies to the work of BorderLinks. The description of the organization's concrete application of its educational endeavors will be seen to follow the projections of Freire's analysis.

Chapter Two

The Dynamics of Education

EVEN THOUGH HE IS frequently thought of as a political activist, Paulo Freire thought of himself as an educator. Initially his work involved developing and implementing educational programs for indigenous peasants in the back country of Brazil. To be sure, such educational endeavors inevitably involved raising the consciousness of those with whom he and his co-workers taught, for people who have learned to read and write are going to see themselves and their world quite differently. It is not surprising that Freire was considered politically dangerous and imprisoned by the Brazilian government. Education is the most effective path to transformation.

The focus of this present chapter will be on Freire's presentation of the pedagogical theory that lies behind his educational vision and practice. Some attention will also be given to certain philosophical ramifications of his theory, as well as to his concrete educational methodology. Along the way the specifics of pedagogical practices employed by BorderLinks will be introduced and correlated with Freire's own insights. In each case it should be borne in mind that this application necessarily involves a basic inversion since on the border those being educated are oppressors rather than the oppressed.

1. Monologue Versus Dialogue

Freire began by contrasting two basic models of the educational process, which he called the banking model and the liberating model. The first of these is familiar enough to nearly everyone who has been educated according to traditional pedagogical methods. Information is presented, it is memorized and banked in the learner's memory for later use when it seems appropriate. The emphasis is on learning the material being taught by those who already possesses the knowledge in question, and on getting everything right as it is presented. Records are kept as to how well the learner has acquired the information in question.

The political results of the banking model of education are that the learners are taught to adapt themselves to the *status quo*, to accept what they are given, and to learn to fit into the way things are. Little or no effort is made to develop the student's consciousness so that they become manageable objects in the system instead of subjects who participate in the cognitive process. "The oppressors use their 'humanitarianism' to preserve a profitable situation. Thus they react almost instinctively against any experiment in education which stimulates the critical faculties and is not content with a partial view of reality."[1]

Clearly this description of the banking approach to education is a bit exaggerated, but anyone who has labored through all those years of grade school, high school, and even many if not most classes in college will be able to relate to the overall dry and confirmative character of traditional Western educational experience. Over against this approach Freire places a liberating pedagogical model which seeks to engage and enliven the minds and behavior of students so that they can and will be full participants in the world and even transformers of it. Rather than seeing the teachers and the students as two ends of a unilateral vector on a continuum, this educational model strives to bring the two together in a co-intentional process in which "both are simultaneously teachers and students."[2] In Freire's approach both students and teachers learn from one another.

Moreover, in this pedagogical partnership both parties direct their attention to the real world around them in order to understand and improve it. The teacher may serve as a kind of elder brother or sister, but it is not assumed that students cannot teach the teacher something new or even contradictory to what he or she believes or thinks. In this co-operative model teachers and students are symbiotically related, or to use Freire's favorite term, they are co-intentional. The stress here is on the interactive process

1. Freire, *Pedagogy*, 73.
2. Freire, *Pedagogy*, 72.

between teachers and learners and between them together and the world around them.

Perhaps Freire's most compact statement of how he sees this mode of the educational dynamic is the following:

> A revolutionary leadership must accordingly practice co-intentional education. Teachers and students (leadership and people), co-intent on reality are both Subjects, not only in the task of unveiling reality, and thereby coming to know it critically, but in the task of recreating that knowledge. As they attain this knowledge through common reflection and action, they discover themselves as permanent re-creators. In this way the presence of the oppressed in the struggle for liberation will be what it should be: not pseudo-participation but committed involvement. [3]

There are two aspects of pedagogy that are essential to its definition and success. The first is its dialogical character and the second is its focus on what Freire calls problem posing. The dialogical aspect has already been discussed in terms of the symbiotic nature of the relationship between students and teachers. In the interactive, liberating model communication is basically dialogical, or truly conversational, in the sense that genuine exchange of ideas and listening to each other's point of view takes place. Beliefs are actually discussed and if need be altered rather than merely rearranged.

The second important aspect of Freire's approach to the educative enterprise pertains to the focus on identifying a few key problems that may have arisen in the context of the lives of the individuals and/or community. Thus rather concentrating on transferring and acquiring information, this pedagogical model zeros in on specific problems that people are actually experiencing presently in the daily lives and on transforming them into something better. Freire puts it this way: "In problem-posing education people develop their own power to perceive critically *the way they exist in the world with which and in which* they find themselves; they come to see the world not as a static reality, but as a reality in process, in transformation. Hence the students-teachers reflect simultaneously on themselves and the world without dichotomizing this reflection from action, and thus establish an authentic form of thought and action."[4]

There are at least two points of connection to be made between Freire's emphases and the insights of other well-known educational thinkers. The

3. Freire, *Pedagogy*, 69.

4. Freire, *Pedagogy*, 83.

first is with that of John Dewey, whose own initially quite radical ideas about the nature of true learning as affected by doing are very similar to Freire's stress on problem-posing. Dewey saw education as an on-going process of confronting and attempting to solve problems. He insisted that the acquisition of information only takes on value from within such practical activity, and that the accepted results of previous cognition are in constant need of updating and overhaul. It is indeed disappointing that Dewey's innovating ideas soon became formalized and fossilized into standard educational practice.

In addition, Freire's emphasis on the integration of the behavioral and intellectual dimensions of human cognition is parallel to that of such phenomenological thinkers as Edmund Husserl and Maurice Merleau-Ponty. Freire actually draws on the work of Husserl when describing the dynamics of consciousness raising in terms of the relationship between our awareness of background and foreground.[5] When one's perceptual horizon is altered what at first was merely background now comes into the foreground and thus into our focal consciousness. Also, Freire's stress on action as an integral aspect of true cognition is similar to Merleau-Ponty's emphasis on the crucial role of the body in all knowing.

Accordingly, the pedagogical posture adopted by BorderLinks in seeking to educate North Americans about the US/Mexico border also focuses on dialogue as contrasted to monologue. Even when experts are called in to inform those participating in a BorderLinks delegation about a specific aspect of the border reality, the format is deliberately set up to stress the role of questions and exchange of ideas. Moreover, within the delegations the discussions and reflections are centered on interaction and full consideration of everyone's point of view.

This is also the case with respect to the way BorderLinks operates when gathered for its bi-monthly staff and board of directors' meetings. When there are decisions to be made all voices must be heard before a consensus is reached. Voting is only resorted to when the matter is pressing and an impasse has arisen. What Quakers call a sense of the meeting is the avowed and practiced goal. Only very few times throughout the organization's existence has it been necessary to resort to the actual voting process in resolving an issue.

It should be noted that the dialogical character of this mode of education befits both the pedagogy of the oppressed and that of the oppressors as well. In both cases the concern is with bringing folks to awareness of

5. Freire, *Pedagogy*, 82–83.

aspects of reality of which they are currently unaware. In addition, the key in both cases is to do so indirectly so as not to confuse, intimidate, or belittle any of those involved. Open, honest dialogue between and among everyone participating in the educative process is the goal. Those arranging such opportunities are, of course, convinced that certain realities about the border hold true, but they also realize that unless those involved come to agree on these beliefs on their own, they will not come to accept them at all.

All of the BorderLinks discussion sessions with members of the various visiting delegations begin by asking the participants to reflect on and share their perceptions and feelings about the experiences of the day or a given document or suggested biblical passage. None of these sharings is ever corrected, even if it seems to be off the mark or beside the point. Generally any such offerings will be off-set by those of another participant, and so genuine dialogue ensues. Sometimes a group leader may direct the group's attention to a different factor in the situation or document that offers an alternative perspective.

Almost invariably this co-intentional procedure results in every member of the delegation being able to see the aspect of the border under consideration in an agreeable manner. The clarity of the situation and the genuine character of the people who are being encountered is generally sufficient to enable participants to understand the border reality for what it is. By creating an arena where visitors to the border can interact with its people and its configurations BorderLinks follows an indirect, inclusive pedagogy similar to that urged by Freire. At least this is the goal, and there is substantial experience that it does in fact take place.

Perhaps two cases in point will serve to illustrate how this methodology works. In one group there was a young man who was convinced that the best approach to border problems is for each country, including the US, simply to mind its own business and stay out of other people's affairs. Through continued discussion with his fellow delegates, and to repeated exposure to information about the magnitude of US corporate and military involvement throughout Latin America, this young man slowly came to admit that such isolationism is neither possible nor desirable.

In a different group there was a young woman who insisted that the only solution to problems like those at the border is a simple one. Everyone simply needs to come to see that all persons must be treated with dignity and fairness, and we must learn to live together as one people on this planet. Several participants in her group sought to explain to her the realities of what some call systemic evil, that when wrong-headed or pernicious decisions and actions become institutionalized they will continue to perpetuate themselves regardless of the best intentions of the individuals involved. The woman finally came to see that socio-political and economic policies must be addressed if justice is going to result.

In concluding this section on the importance of dialogue in the educative process, especially as it is applies to the programs and projects of BorderLinks, it may prove helpful to point out that even at the level of staff and board meetings, every effort is made to follow a dialogical pattern. From the very beginning the founder and director of BorderLinks, Rick Ufford-Chase insisted that every decision making process follow a format of full and open conversation about each major issue, and this has remained the pattern throughout the years the organization has been in existence.

There have been several occasions, both in staff meetings and on board meetings, when the organizational leadership has come to the table with specific projects or proposals and has presented them to the group with enthusiasm, only to have one or two members of the group raise serious questions about the appropriateness or feasibility of the ideas presented. On at least two occasions large-scale building proposals, which were the pet projects of the director himself, were set aside because the consensus was against them.

In one of these instances the objection had to do with the proposed project involving more money, time, and energy than the organization could currently afford. In another instance one person objected that it did not seem right to put money into buildings rather than into programs, and the group came to agree with this objection. On both of these occasions not only did the leadership acquiesce without complaining, but it later turned out that a better way of accomplishing what had initially been proposed revealed itself and was undertaken. It is important that BorderLinks practices what it preaches in seeking to follow Freire's understanding of transformational pedagogy, even and perhaps especially at the leadership level.

2. Problem-Posing Education

As was mentioned in the previous section, problem-posing as a pedagogical method goes hand-in-hand with a dialogical approach. Freire almost always speaks of the two in connection with each other and actually seems to see them as two sides of the same reality. The dialogical format replaces the familiar lecture-monologue format as a pedagogical technique, while the problem-posing pattern replaces the traditional act of transferring information as the educational procedure. Together these two symbiotic dimensions constitute the heart of Freire's understanding of true cognitive activity.

In essence, the problem-posing educational method begins, not with the teacher's knowledge and information, but with those problems which the learners themselves are facing in their everyday lives. At times it is useful, to be sure, for the teacher to call attention to or focus a given problem in order to get dialogue underway. Freire expresses it this way:

> The teacher presents the material to the students for their consideration, and reconsiders her earlier considerations as the students express their own. The role of the problem-posing educator increasingly critical and thus constantly less alienated is to create, together with the students, the conditions under which knowledge at the level of *doxa* is superseded by true knowledge at the level of *logos* . . . Students as they are increasingly posed with problems relating to themselves in the world, will feel increasingly challenged and obliged to respond to the challenge. Because they apprehend the challenge as interrelated with other problems within a total context, not as a theoretical question, the resulting comprehension tends to be increasingly critical and thus constantly less alienated.[6]

As with the emphasis on a dialogical method, the emphasis on a problem-posing approach completely redefines the relation between teacher and student. Instead of a vertical and unilateral relation from teacher to student, there now exists a more horizontal and bilateral relation in which teacher and student mutually inform and challenge each other to think ever more creatively and critically. It is focusing on specific problems that brings this relational transformation about, since there are no preconceived pieces of information for the teacher to dispense at the outset, even though such data may well prove useful at a later point in the discussion. As Freire puts it:

> The teacher is no longer merely the-one-who-teaches, but one who is himself taught in dialogue with the students, who while being taught will also teach. They become jointly responsible for a process in which they all grow. In this process arguments based on 'authority' are no longer valid; in order to function, authority must be on the *side* of freedom, and not *against* it. Here, no one teaches another, nor is anyone self-taught. People teach each other,

---

6. Freire, *Pedagogy*, 81.

mediated by the world, by the cognizable objects which in banking education are owned by the teacher. [7]

There are two obvious difficulties which can arise in this approach rendering it far less than effective. One of these pertains to the student's lack of confidence in relation to the one who is supposed to be the teacher. It frequently happens that students are both intimidated and frustrated by the possibility of entering into a more egalitarian relationship with an authority figure. Freire quotes from two separate occasions in which peasants who had been invited to participate in a dialogical educational process, objected to the idea. The one interrupted and said: "'Excuse us, we ought to keep quiet and let you talk. You are the one who knows. We don't know anything.' The second simply began by asking: 'Why don't you explain the pictures first? That will take less time and won't give us a headache.'" [8]

It is, of course, extremely important to work at creating an atmosphere and dynamic that enables a person to get beyond this sort of intimidation. In some ways this issue lies at the core of the sort of education Freire is promoting, since once a person feels comfortable with and challenged by this opportunity, the task is essentially accomplished. Learning to learn is really what the whole pedagogical process is about. Moreover, unless this initial hurdle can be leaped, nothing else can really be done.

The second danger that can arise with the problem-posing approach occurs when the teacher or teachers involved simply are unable to relinquish the position of authority. Unfortunately, this difficulty comes into play far too frequently and may in fact be harder to avoid. After all, those who have been invested with pedagogical authority, after investing years of study and making many sacrifices, naturally feel they are entitled to a position of acknowledged leadership. To actually admit to learning from students is asking a lot. Here is how Freire analyzes this difficulty:

> Unfortunately, those who espouse the cause of liberation are themselves surrounded and influenced by the climate which generates the banking concept, and often do not perceive its true significance or its dehumanizing power. Paradoxically, then, they utilize this same instrument of alienation in what they consider an effort to liberate. Indeed, some 'revolutionaries' brand as 'innocents,' 'dreamers,' or even 'reactionaries' those who would challenge this educational practice. But one does not liberate people

7. Freire, *Pedagogy*, 80.

8. Freire, *Pedagogy*, 63.

by alienating them. Authentic liberation, the process of human-
ization, is not another deposit to be made in people. Liberation
is a praxis: the action and reflection men and women upon their
world in order to transform it. Those truly committed to the cause
of liberation can accept neither the mechanistic concept of consciousness as an empty vessel to be filled, nor the use of banking
methods of domination (propaganda, slogans, deposits) in the
name of liberation. [9]

 As an example of the sort of problem-posing educational process of
which Freire speaks, consider the way a particular college history department chose to structure its introductory course. Rather than beginning
with various surveys of traditional time periods and geographical areas, this
department began with a course entitled What Is History? In this course
students sought out answers to this question by examining the process by
means of which what we call history actually gets written. They analyzed
documents, compiled oral histories, and generally came to understand
what history as a discipline really is. Cataloging information came later on.

 A third characteristic of problem-posing education is that it is action
oriented rather than being passive in nature. Not only does a person learn
by doing, as John Dewey forcefully emphasized, but all true learning even-
tuates in behavioral activity. Freire repeatedly uses the notion of praxis to
convey what he has in mind here. The term derives from such European
dialectical thinkers as Hegel, Marx, and Lukacs. It basically designates
intentional action informed by rational reflection. As he insists, thought
without action quickly degenerates into mere verbalism, while action without thought results in simplistic activism.

 As he puts it himself: "In dialectical thought, world and action are
intimately interdependent. But action is human only when it is not merely
an occupation but also a preoccupation, that is, when it is not dichotomized
from reflection. Reflection, which is essential to action is implicit in Lukacs'
requirement of 'explaining to the masses their own action,' just as it is implicit in the purpose he attributes to this explanation: that of 'consciously
activating the subsequent development of experience.'"[10]

 All of which means that only through conscious reflection on a situation, and his or her place in it, can a person actually participate in grasping
and shaping the surrounding world, both now and in the future. Praxis is the

9. Freire, *Pedagogy*, 74.
10. Freire, *Pedagogy*, 53.

synthesis of thought and action put to humanizing and liberating use. Without this reflective process on one's experience, on the one hand, it remains a mere passive phenomenon, while on the other hand, without it one's action becomes mere busyness at best and downright fool-hardy at worst.

When it comes to outlining how BorderLinks implements the foregoing principles and techniques, a lot has already been said in our first chapter, as well as in the previous section of this present chapter. Along with introducing its visitors to the people and dynamics of the US/Mexico border, BorderLinks schedules frequent opportunities for discussions of what they have been experiencing and how it makes them feel. The problems confronting those living on the border are put before the groups and conversations concerning what causes these problems and what might be done about them naturally ensue.

Moreover, BorderLinks has always been concerned about what its staff has regularly called the "So what?"—question. That is to say, once the group participants have visited the border and returned to their homes and communities, what can be expected of them? How can BorderLinks better facilitate some sort of follow-up empowerment for these folks so that they can really make a difference in their everyday lives and in the lives of others where they live and work? Plans have always been underway and are always developing for the organization to become more concrete in his area of the organization's educational enterprise.

It is not surprising that significantly more can be done and is being done in this respect within the academic dimension of BorderLinks educational programs. For here there is more time and opportunity to delve deeper into the issues involved and to explore possible solutions, both to the problems facing people on the border and to those facing other North Americans as they endeavor to be more responsive and faithful to what they have learned. Some college and seminary groups come to BorderLinks for as many as three weeks at a time, often bring their own faculty member and providing their own credit from their home institution. Often these groups hold their own regular study sessions using selected books and their own current experiences of the problems confronting people on the border.

In its own Semester on the Border program BorderLinks is connected with a half dozen colleges and universities around the country which send students for a full semester, providing their own academic credit and using BorderLinks professors as their adjunct faculty. The course of studies offers full college level courses in Spanish, Peace and Justice Studies, History of

Mexico, Liberation Theology, and Philosophy of Culture. The students divide their time equally between living on the US side and the Mexican side of the border, where they do four week homestays with Mexican families.

This program provides concrete time and opportunity for the examination of the problems posed by the border realities and what might be done about them. In fact, most of the daily class sessions begin by discussing students' sparker papers with which students zero-in on specific issues raised by the textbooks in relation to their own border experience. The methodology here is aimed at real dialogue between and among students and teachers, with a great deal of emphasis placed on discussion, paper and journal writing, as well as project presentations. Toward the close of the semester the students naturally begin to focus on problems they will face upon returning to their schools and homes with the new, fresh perspective provided by their border experience.

The faculty for this semester program involves an experienced PhD professor in philosophy and religious studies, a PhD graduate student at the University of Arizona in Mexican History, as well a graduate student in Spanish. The aim is to find people who combine both an in-depth yet progressively-aimed knowledge of their field with practical knowledge of the border reality. These faculty are all accredited by each college or university granting the credits for the semester students.

Another dimension to the BorderLinks application of the problem-posing pedagogical pattern was added when it was decided to put together a celebration for the organization's tenth anniversary in 1998. The planning for this event ran, as one might expect, with many different people and voices involved in various brain-storming sessions. Rather than simply bring a large number of alumni and supporters together for a standard sort of conference, the plan evolved to sponsor several different week-long travel seminars to some Central American countries, as well as to the US/Mexico border, using them as fact-finding experiences for a weekend consultation.

These travel seminars provided the celebration/consultation with ample input for discussions concerning the current states of affairs in these different locals at that time, the problems they were facing and what was and still could be done about them. The consultation started off on a Friday evening with the keynote address by an activist catholic Bishop Thomas Gumbleton, from Detroit. Then on Saturday morning participants of the various travel seminars took turns sharing what they saw and found in the places they visited. The problems facing the people living in those places were clearly posed for all the participants.

The focus of the consultation shifted in the afternoon to what North Americans can do about the situations in Central America and on the border, thereby posing another set of concrete problems for the participants. Saturday evening was devoted to celebrating through feasting, dancing, and singing. Sunday afternoon and Monday morning saw many different small groups networking and planning future actions, many of which actually came to pass in subsequent months and years. There were actually plans being laid for the up-coming twenty year celebrations in years to come.

This entire event followed Freire's outline of the nature of problem-posing education to the letter. The initial planning stage was a problem-posing one, followed by action. The travel seminars focused on problems in Central America and the border and proposed some specific solutions, and even began making plans for further involvement. In every case those who led the consultations and those who attended worked together in dialogue and praxis in finding ways to transform their common reality.

One final illustration of BorderLinks' implementation of Freire's pedagogical methodology came in connection with the need for a consultant who could guide the organization through the growing pains it was experiencing as a result of recent rapid expansion of staff, programs, and fund raising. A consultant was located, a professor of growth management who gave her time and wisdom without charge, and a series of staff retreats were held under her leadership to deal with these problems. Through dialogue, sharing, and role-playing the BorderLinks staff was enabled to focus its difficulties and find a working solution to them.

This same dynamic was what triggered the idea of establishing a Board of Directors back in 1995. Up until that time the director simply made basic decisions after consulting with key members of the staff and local advisors. A friend of Rick Ufford-Chase, who was widely experienced in the business world was asked to be the main consultant in the process of setting up the Board of Directors, and things did, of course, begin to work more smoothly thereafter. Even though BorderLinks found it necessary, due to much appreciated growth, to shift from a strictly consensual way of doing business to a collegial model, the actual dynamics of decision making has not changed all that much. Problems are posed and decisions are made in a collegial manner at different levels of the organization and no longer need to involve the entire organization in the process. Dialogue is still the guiding principle and action is still the goal.

3. Language Creates Reality

Before turning to a more detailed treatment of the specific techniques that Paulo Freire employed in his efforts to educate various oppressed peoples, and to the ways in which BorderLinks seeks to adapt these, albeit in inverted fashion, to the education of North Americans about the US/Mexico border, some attention needs to be given to one other more or less abstract issue. Although this issue may at first seem irrelevant to the main concerns of this present exploration of pedagogical principles, it actually lies at the very center, for it deals with the question of locating the axis around which these principles actually revolve.

Freire devotes a considerable amount of space in chapter three to a reflection on the nature of the relationship between language and reality. His focus is on the fact that frequently the words we use to describe and understand a given aspect of the world around us actually help to form the very character of that reality. In Freire's view, the relationship between words and the world is not an arbitrary, merely conventional one, but often carries a great deal of power to create and transform the world in which we live.

He begins with an analysis of the word 'dialogue' itself, since this constitutes the very heart of his educational methodology. Derived from the Greek, the word dialogue means through or by means of speech and or reasoning. Freire contends that this term designates a process consisting of two symbiotic poles or foci: "Within the word we find two dimensions, reflection and action, in such radical interaction that if one is sacrificed— even in part—the other immediately suffers. There is no true word that is not at the same time a praxis. Thus to speak a word is to transform the world."[11] This emphasis on the active, or what the philosopher J.L. Austin termed the performative character of linguistic activity sets in motion a whole new perspective on the nature of the relationship between human speech and the natural as well as the social world.

Until recently it was generally assumed, both by lay folk and philosophers that language functions as a kind of mirror or picture of the way things are in the world. Thus, for instance, the word 'white' describes or labels the color of this piece of paper, while the word 'paper' stands for, or

11. Freire, *Pedagogy*, 87.

names, this white object. In recent decades, however, it has become increasingly clear that the relationship between language and the world is far more complex than this picture model will allow. The actual meaning of a word, or any linguistic expression, is a function of its use, and this changes from one context to another.

For instance, at first glance we may think that the expression "the door is open" pictures or describes a state of affairs with respect to a door. The word 'door' stands for that object over there and the term 'open' pictures its present condition, namely not closed. It only takes a second, however, to see that there are many uses to which this simple expression can and is frequently put. I may say to my friend who is hesitant about facing a new opportunity: "Go ahead, the door is open." Or the director of a company may wish to encourage employees to drop by for a visit by saying: "Come on by, the door is open."

Things can get even more complex. The parent of a child that consistently leaves the door open may use the expression "the door is open" as an imperative to tell the child to go close the door. Or, to take another example, a philosophy professor may continually use the statement merely as an example, even when the class meets outside, where there is no door at all. Indeed, students who are sick and tired of this example may use it as a kind of joke or greeting whenever they meet crossing the campus.

The philosopher J.L. Austin analyzed this multi-dimensional character of language in terms of what he called its performative character, referred to such acts as speech-acts, which have three different though simultaneous dimensions or forces. First there is the linguistic expression itself. Second there is the purpose or intent for which the speaker spoke the words. And third there is the response the words elicit, which may be quite different from that intended. The point here is that language is far more complex than we usually think. It is poly-significant or multi-dimensional.

For instance, we generally do not realize the emotional or political effect that words have. Calling a woman a 'girl,' or an African American man a 'boy' carries with it a great deal of emotional or social significance. There was a fine film about a child whose birth came rather late in the parents' life and so they called him 'PS.' The child felt diminished by his nick name because he felt he had been conceived as an after-thought. As the saying has it today: "Words matter."

It is the powerful performative quality of language that Freire picks up on in his work. He focuses on the naming function, not in the sense of mere labelling, but in the sense that when someone has the power to designate what the different features of the world are to be called, that person, like Orpheus, actually calls the world into being and creates its qualities. Freire's point is that the oppressed do not get to name their own reality, do not participate in making the world in which they live. It is the ruling class that names reality.

Thus the pedagogy of the oppressed consists in enabling them to be in a position to think of themselves as ones who are capable of transforming their own world. Cleary learning to read and write goes a long way toward helping to make this a reality in the lives of dispossessed peoples, for literacy opens up unlimited possibilities. Oppressed people may thus learn better to see their own place in the world when it is objectified before them in photos, drawings, and role-playing situations. Indeed, they may come to be able actually identify or name various aspects of their reality in much the same way small children come to see various physical aspects of the world and call out their names in recognition of the fact that they are coming to understand how the world is put together. Here is the way Freire expresses this insight:

> To exist humanly is to *name* the world, to change it. Once named the world in its turn reappears to the namers as a problem and requires of them a new naming. Human beings are not built in silence, but in word, in work, in action-reflection. But while to say the true word—which is work, which is praxis—is to transform the world, saying that word is not the privilege of some few persons, but the right of everyone. Consequently no one can say a true word alone—nor can she *say* it for another, in a prescriptive act which robs others of their words. Dialogue is the encounter between men, mediated by the world, in order to name the world. [12]

In the same way as children who are beginning to acquire their native language are told what sounds to associate with which objects, qualities, and actions, what things are for and whose they are, so too are oppressed people told what things belong to whom, how they should think and act, and who gets to call the plays. Oppressed people are born into a world that they had nothing to do with creating, and thus they simply absorb its structure and values without thinking that things could be different, that they could change, that is rename their reality.

---

12. Freire, *Pedagogy*, 88.

Freire tells of a peasant who gave voice to the insight that without people to name the world there would be no world. When asked if the world would not still exist even if there were no human beings in it, the man replied: "Oh no. There would be no one to say: 'This is the world.'"[13] Also Freire points out how oppressors help create the oppressed by speaking of them as "those people," "savages," "subversives," and the like, even if they never call them "the oppressed." Of course, oppressors would never think of calling themselves "the oppressors."

This discussion of the creative power of language in helping to structure reality, is of course highly relevant to the contemporary debate about the importance of politically correct speech. Within the context of Freire's analysis what is crucial here is that a person or cultural group should have the right to decide for themselves how they want to be referred to, or more accurately, they should be able to name themselves. This after all is the critical point at the center of this whole political debate about racism. If African American people want to be called Negroes, or Blacks, they should have the right and the empowerment to expect the rest of society to honor this wish. The same applies to the terms for women: ladies, women, and girls. Women have the right to choose their label.

The difficulty has been that down through the years those in the positions of power have named the world, including the different people in it, and have done so for their own convenience and advantage. All of the derogatory terms for foreigners and disadvantaged groups have come about in this way. It is past high-time that people be given the opportunity to speak for themselves with regard to how they wish to be addressed. Being politically correct is not merely a matter of not offending other persons or cultural groups, but of seeing to it that all peoples have the right and the power to name themselves. The key to making this possibility is to have dialogue between and amongst various individuals and groups so that a context of mutual respect and understanding can prevail. Such dialogue is, unfortunately, often as difficult as it is important to achieve.

Ironically, and sadly enough, the point Freire is making was forcefully illustrated in the very language he employed in writing his book. Throughout the original edition of his *Pedagogy of the Oppressed* Freire used the traditional gender specific grammatical forms of his native tongue, such as 'mankind,' 'men,' and 'man' when speaking of humankind in general. Clearly one of the most oppressed people of the world, especially in Latin

13. Freire, *Pedagogy*, 82.

America, are women, and quite to Freire's point with respect to his own way of speaking, specifically the naming of the world, this fact is still the dominant way of naming reality throughout the world.

Fortunately, the thirtieth anniversary edition of his book from which all the quotations in this present volume have been taken, were corrected so as to reflect the main thrust of Freire's overall point in these passages. Since it was edited after Freire's death in 1997 it is not clear whether he himself had anything to do with this updating. Be that as it may, his main point stands that the way reality gets named, and by whom, strongly influences its shape and content. Moreover, the oppressed of the world have, until recently, largely been left out of the naming process. I should think that Freire himself would surely agree.

One final illustration. The term 'revolution' takes on quite distinctive and contrary meanings depending on whether it is used in the context of the American Revolution in 1776 or in the context of various modern or contemporary revolutions such as those in Russia, Cuba, Nicaragua, or China. In the former case it has a positive spin, while in the latter cases the spin is clearly a negative one. As they say, history is written by the winners because they get to name the world. A while back the advertisements for Chevrolet cars employed the term 'revolution' in order to trade off of its positive spin. When applied to things pertaining to the US the term is viewed positively by Americans, but when applied to what people of other countries in order to achieve justice and freedom for themselves it is often viewed negatively by Americans.

Freire completes his treatment of the relation between language and reality by reemphasizing the critical nature of dialogue and its role in the naming process. Specifically, he spells out the parameters that render dialogue possible: love, humility, faith, and hope. What he says about the importance of love applies with equal force to the other characteristics as well:

"Dialogue cannot exist, however, in the absence of a profound love for the world and for people. The naming of the world, which is an act of creation and recreation, is not possible if it is not infused with love. Love is at the same time the foundation of dialogue and dialogue itself. It is thus necessarily the task of responsible Subjects and cannot exist in a relation of domination. Domination reveals the pathology of love: sadism in the dominator and masochism in the dominated."[14]

14. Freire, *Pedagogy*, 89.

Thus it is that the pivotal part played by language in the pedagogy of the oppressed, as well as that in the pedagogy of the oppressors, can now be more fully appreciated. True dialogue, which is the fulcrum of all real education, is mediated in and through language, which makes it the axis of any effort to liberate the oppressed. As Freire says, a failure to understand the power and integrity of language will cause all revolutionary movements to deteriorate into mere slogan and propaganda mongers.[15] It is absolutely crucial to understand these seemingly abstract concepts if one is going to be able to comprehend the nature of the relationship between the oppressed and the oppressors. Education is the key to liberation, dialogue is the key to education, and authentic language is the key to dialogue.

Even though the issue of the relationship between language and reality has never been a conscious concern in the day-to-day operation of the BorderLinks organization, it has, nonetheless, played an important role in the choice of vocabulary used by those working therein. For, how one speaks to and about those with whom one is working along the US/Mexico border makes a great deal of difference at many levels. Even the name BorderLinks carries with it certain nuances of meaning that some other name would not.

For example, some years back a young Mexican woman good humoredly objected to the way North Americans use the terms 'America' and 'United States' as if there were no other countries in the Western hemisphere. Mexico, too, along with the nations of Central and South America, is part of the Americas. And it too is a union of individual states. It is more than just interesting to note that a great many countries in the world are not referred to by the people of other countries by the name which they use for themselves. Germany, Greece, Spain, and the Scandinavian countries are good examples. Even many Native American tribes are referred to by Anglos with the names given to them by the Spaniards or even by their enemies.

When talking about the communities in Nogales, Sonora, MX, with whom BorderLinks works, it is important to choose one's words carefully. The terms 'squatter village,' 'shanty town,' and especially 'slums,' carry heavy negative connotations that strongly color our thinking about the people who dwell in such places. A more preferred designation is *colonia*, since it is the term the people themselves use. Even the term 'land invasion' to refer to how many of these communities got underway is quite acceptable since it is one of the terms the people living there often use themselves.

15. Freire, *Pedagogy*, 37–40.

All of these considerations fall under what Freire means by the concept of naming. Who gets to name the world is every bit as crucial on the border as it is anywhere else where oppressed people are pushed to the margins of their own society. There is, for instance, a special irony in the name for the political party that ruled Mexico for over seventy years, the PRI. These initials stand for the words Institutionalized Revolutionary Party, an oxymoron if there ever was one. In fact, it is doubly ironic that a party so full of corruption and authoritarian rule should designate itself revolutionary in character.

When it comes to BorderLinks itself, there have been a number of cases in which the naming process has been significant. When the board of directors was initially established, the membership felt quite uncomfortable with this designation and decided to call itself the steering committee. Even the chairperson prefers to be called the coordinator of the steering committee. The same holds true for other coordinators of various dimensions of the organization. This all may seem silly, but as Freire says, the world will become and will be dealt with according to the way we name it. "Words matter." As you name it, so shall it be.

Even the question of how one addresses the people with whom one works reflects this issue of the importance of the naming dynamic. Spanish names are sometimes difficult to get right in terms of pronunciation and spelling, but it is very important to work at doing so, since any person's name is of deep emotional significance to them. To tag a person with a nickname because their proper name is elusive or difficult to pronounce simply will not do. Also, titles of respect, such as *Doña* for an older woman and *Don* for an older man can be very helpful in establishing a working relationship.

From the very beginning BorderLinks has striven to be as bilingual as possible, requiring that all of its delegation leaders, both Mexican and US, be fluent in both Spanish and English. In addition, all of the staff and steering committee meetings make use of both languages, with either simultaneous translation equipment or alternating direct translation. By paying attention to such details the organization seeks to create the reality it aspires to, one in which all people receive full respect and dignity regardless of race, gender, or nationality.

Turning to the ways in which North Americans often speak about Mexicans or Latin Americans in the US, it comes as no surprise that there is a great deal to be learned in this regard. Setting aside altogether the standard slang words and worse, even the terms 'migrant,' 'illegal,' and 'homeless' can be misleading and demeaning. 'Immigrant,' 'undocumented,' and 'refugee' would be less offensive and more useful designations. This issue has recently become increasingly important as a result of the millions of undocumented Mexicans now working in the US, together with the political uproar waking up to this state of affairs has caused throughout the country.

Finally, some attention should be given to the ways one speaks about oppressors themselves. Clearly, no one is likely to be pleased by being called an oppressor. This is perhaps the most difficult aspect of discussing pedagogy of the oppressor, since it requires some way to address all of these issues in a manner that truly raises consciousness and conscience without alienating and causing a person to become defensive. Even terms like 'ruling class,' 'privileged class,' and 'dominant culture' are far from neutral and may well even be counter-productive with respect to transforming the minds of North Americans.

Perhaps it would be best to try to avoid all such terminology and simply speak about what is seen, heard, and, felt. In the work that BorderLinks does, every effort is made to keep from prejudicing and pressuring in any one direction with regard to the political and moral issues involved at the US/Mexico border. At the same time, however, it remains true that the conditions on the border are not the result of accidental causes, and it is part and parcel of BorderLinks mission to highlight and examine the why and wherefore of this reality. Poverty is neither a natural nor accidental phenomenon, it is the direct or indirect result of specific political and economic policies.

This is the real meaning of experiential learning that BorderLinks uses to describe its endeavors. The assumption is that by bringing North Americans to the border, and arranging for them to experience it first-hand in the context of honest and open discussion with others who care about the issues, a transformative dynamic will naturally be set in motion. Seeing and reflecting will hopefully lead to action. Most Americans are struck dumb, both by the abject poverty they encounter at the border, and by the positive attitude with which those living this reality respond to their own situation.

4. Getting Specific

It is now time to give attention to the specific techniques used by Paulo Freire in his educative activities with oppressed people in Latin America. Although a general sense of how he went about the actual pedagogical process can be gained from the foregoing treatment of his overall vision, an account of his particular methods will be even more helpful in acquiring a thorough understanding of Freire's radical educational and political philosophy. That it was and is a radical pedagogy is testified to by the fact that Freire was jailed more than once for engaging in his efforts to help make his fellow Brazilian peasants literate, both in terms of knowledge and practice.

The basic thrust of Freire's approach is well summed up in the following remarks:

> The starting point for organizing the program content for political action must be the present, existential concrete situation, reflecting the aspirations of the people. Utilizing certain basic contradictions, we must pose the existential, concrete situation to the people as a problem which challenges them and requires a response—not just at the intellectual level, but at the level of action.[16]

Freire goes on to stress the importance of language in this understanding of the starting point of all such work. He observes that often educators and politicians alike are very much out of touch of where the people they speak to and with whom they work really are in their everyday lives. It is crucial that one's terminology and style of speech be in tune with that of the people, for otherwise no real communication will take place. Often intellectuals use jargon and politicians use meaningless word-salad that the common people do not understand.

From the outset Freire makes it clear that the real focus of his work was laying bare what he calls the thematic universe that defines the thought life of and shapes the behavior of those whom one is seeking to educate. He states that this universe or worldview is composed of generative themes that together constitute the contours and texture of everyday life for any given people, in this case for oppressed peoples. This world is, indeed, generated according to various themes or paradigms that serve as the warp and weft of any given cultural fabric. To change the metaphor, these themes are the matrix or womb out of which any given reality is born.

These themes are what might be termed the joints of a people's concrete situation, and thus they lie open on the surface of community life, but must be revealed or laid bare by means of the dialogical educative process already discussed in the previous sections of this chapter. They must be brought to the surface by means of interactive discussion, with an eye toward action and transformation within the world where oppressed people

16. Freire, *Pedagogy*, 95.

live and work. Freire's actual pedagogical practices aim at precisely this sort of dialogical interaction.

The different ways that these themes assert and express themselves make up what Freire, borrowing from Professor Alvaro Vieira Pinto calls limit-situations, the actual lived context of the people in question. While these limiting factors do in fact define and confine oppressed people, everything depends on how they are perceived by the people themselves. Freire says: "Thus it is not the limit situations in and of themselves which create a climate of hopelessness, but rather how they are perceived by women and men at a given historical moment: whether they appear as fetters or as insurmountable barriers."[17] These limit-situations powerfully reflect and embody the various generative themes making up a given people's world. They can be represented as concentric circles moving from the general to the particular. Freire states: "I consider the fundamental theme of our epoch to be that of *domination*—which implies its opposite, the theme of *liberation,* as the objective to be achieved."[18] At the more specific level he finds *development* and *underdevelopment*, both of which hinge on the notion of dependency, to be crucial in defining the limit-situations.

According to Freire the entire context within which people live exerts itself in each situation in the form of a code which an educator needs to help people decode so they can understand their world, their place in it, and what can be done about it. The decoding process can be seen at work in North American culture when one analyses an advertisement so as to be able to see through it, or behind it. "You've come a long way, baby!" for instance hides the fact that women comparatively remain well behind men in our society, and that they are not babies. Also, the cigarette ad that says: "Be you, be Cooper!" decodes into "Let us tell you who you are and what you should do," namely: "Buy Cooper cigarettes."

The dynamic involved in this decoding process amounts to finding ways with which to objectify the lived experience of the people so that they can come to see their own lives from the outside, as it were. Freire insists that it is not the people themselves that are of interest here, but rather, it is the situation within which they exist in relation to one another and the world around them. It is not, in Freire's view, individual objects or people that comprise reality, but it is the relationships between and among them.

17. Freire, *Pedagogy,* 99.

18. Freire, *Pedagogy,* 103.

These interactive relationships follow patterns and need to be decoded so that the reality in which oppressed people live can be revealed.

The first stage of this pedagogical procedure involves establishing initial contacts with the people and explaining how and why the educational enterprise will proceed. Individual volunteers are asked to serve as assistants in the gathering of information about how the community functions. Then the educational team, acting as anthropological investigators, circulate in the village, gathering data about its life and culture, collecting concrete examples of behavior that express this reality for future decoding. Freire describes this process thusly:

> It is essential that the investigators observe the area under varying circumstances: labor in the fields, meetings of a local association (noting the behavior of the participants, the language used, and the relations between the officers and the members), the role played by women and young people, leisure hours, games and sports, conversations with people in their homes (noting examples of husband/wife and parent/child relationships). No activity must be allowed to escape the attention of the investigators during the initial survey of the area. [19]

After the investigators share and discuss their findings, revising them as seems appropriate, they are ready to begin the second phase of their work.

The foci of this second phase of the educative process are various contradictions that appear within the fabric of the communities' life that reveal the generative themes and limit-situations thereof. "Always acting as a team, the investigators will select some of these contradictions to develop the codifications to be used in the thematic investigation. Since the codifications (sketches or photographs) are the *objects* which mediate the decoders in their critical analysis, they must represent situations familiar to the individuals whose thematics are being examined and they must be neither overly explicit nor overly enigmatic."[20]

In the process of decoding their own community life and individual behavior, the participants externalize the themes comprising the warp and weft of their shared situation and worldview. They not only come to see themselves behaving in certain ways, but they become aware of their own perceptions of their observed behavior, and thereby achieve a kind of

19. Freire, *Pedagogy*, 111–12.

20. Freire, *Pedagogy*, 114–15.

self-transcendence about their lives and values. During this whole process the educators both listen to and challenge the people by posing problems that arise from what they say and do. This procedure enables the people to objectify observations and feelings they might not have even been aware of, let alone express in a different context.

Freire explicitly contrasts this more inductive approach to eliciting information and self-understanding to that of most traditional education wherein the teacher often imposes a prearranged agenda on the learners. He provides many concrete examples of how this concrete, story-related objectifying procedure opens the people's eyes to what is going on in their own lives and to the contradictions therein. Freire offers an insightful example of how this more indirect process works with the following story.

"In one of the thematic investigations carried out in Santiago, a group of tenement residents discussed a scene showing a drunken man walking on the street and three young men conversing on the corner. The group participants commented that 'the only one there who is productive and useful to his country is the souse who is returning home after working all day for low wages and who is worried about his family because he can't take care of their needs. He is the only worker. He is a decent worker and a souse like us.'"[21]

Freire goes on to analyze these comments as revealing an important contradiction in the men's lives, one between understanding the frustrations of a hard working yet exploited worker and his self-destructive behavior, on the one hand, and rating him higher than the young men who only stand around and talk, on the other. It is these photographs and drawings of their everyday lives that enable the people to see themselves objectified and acknowledge aspects of their lives which they normally overlook. This is the very heart of Freire's methodology.

The third stage of the investigation involves the investigators completing a systematic and interdisciplinary study of their findings. But the real work centers in the process of the participants coming to understand their own situation and beginning to feel that they can do something about it. To be able to see and hear themselves in concrete situations, together with the contradictions that are revealed thereby, provides them with genuine insight into their own situation. In addition, this fresh understanding has come about through the dialogical interaction with other people who live in the same situations and experience life as oppressed and exploited.

21. Freire, *Pedagogy*, 118.

Once again it is time to turn to a consideration of how the specifics of Paolo Freire's pedagogical techniques can be applied to the task of educating North Americans as to the realities of the US/Mexico border. Here again we face the difficult job of inverting his principles from a focus of educating the oppressed to that of educating the oppressors. The axis of Freire's approach is the presentation of the lives of the people in question in a way that enables them to see themselves and their situation in a new and transforming fashion. He accomplished this by the use of photographs and drawings of the people's activities, together with their own descriptions of and responses to them.

One of the primary ways that participants in BorderLinks programs come to experience something similar to this is by returning home. That is to say, after having been immersed, if only briefly, in the realities of life on the border, it is always a shock to return to one's own life and work. The contrast between the two is almost always overwhelming. Our own abundance and wastefulness, our compulsion to consume, and our lack of understanding of how other people live, largely because of how we in the privileged class demand that we live, go a long way toward helping North Americans see themselves more objectively.

One follow-up technique that some folks use to provide themselves with an objective view of the life of oppressors is to take a week, or even a day, to experiment with just how much one can do without. Try living without TV, with only one (or no) car, and without heat or air-conditioning, to say nothing of cell phones, for just a day. This sort of experiment can serve as a profound wake-up call for those of us North Americans who take our over-privileged life style for granted, even as something to which we are entitled. There are, in addition, far too many people in our country who live without the basics, let alone the conveniences, to which we have come to think that we deserve, such as the homeless, the folks on reservations, and those living in slums or on the streets of our major cities. Spending time with such folks serves to change one's view of one's own lifestyle and value system.

BorderLinks employs several concrete opportunities for its participants to have a chance to experience themselves and their own level of life in an objectified manner. After having completed a visit to the border and its people, most groups finish up their trip by processing together in a sharing and reflection session. Here various observations and questions are discussed, and individuals often see themselves and their colleagues in a quite different light. In addition, sometimes participants are encouraged to put what they have experienced in a drawing or a poem.

One young man told of watching TV with his host family when an ad came on the screen for *White Magic*, a cream for Mexican people to put on their skin to make it lighter in tone. He said that he was so embarrassed that he had to go outside. His face became so red that he actually became unbearably hot. Even as he told this story he had obviously become very uncomfortable and made his colleagues uncomfortable as well. These participants clearly saw themselves in him and realized that even their own skin served as an expression of their privileged existence, if only to themselves.

Another technique that BorderLinks uses is that of role-playing simulation games in which trip participants play the roles of various oppressed peoples and thus see themselves from a quite different perspective. One of these games is called the Immigration Skit and in it participants act out various aspects of the immigration process, from trying to cross the border legally, to trying to sneak across illegally, and finally to getting caught and deported. The standing in endless lines, paying fees, as well as bribes, waiting months for a visa, crawling over and under walls and fences, paying a *coyote*, or a smuggler to lead you across the border, getting lost and/or left by him, running from the border patrol, and finally getting deported.

Acting out all this brings home the repression many Mexicans experience and serves to raise North American consciousness about the nature of the US border policies, especially when one realizes that all of this effort that the Mexican folk expend is in reality only an attempt to find work and support their families. Almost all of those that do make it into the US find work, pay taxes, and return home within eight years. They do not become homeless or criminals, nor are they a drain on our economy, because mostly they take jobs that American workers refuse.

It should not go unmentioned in this context that hundreds of migrants die trying to cross into the US. The high concentration of border patrol in and near the cities along the border makes it necessary for them to sneak across in remote desert areas where they often die from exposure to excessive heat in the summer or cold in the winter. For a helpful and timeless analysis of these issues the reader is encouraged to see the June 11, 2001 issue of Time Magazine. Although the participants in BorderLinks delegations are not themselves responsible for establishing and/or maintaining the US border policy, exposure to its results in the lives of Mexican people provides yet another means of seeing ourselves as others people see us. For a moving and personalized story of one individual's traumatic experience the reader is encouraged to watch a film by Chris Weitz called *A Better Life*.

A second game often played by those on BorderLinks trips is called the Debt Skit and it aims at an understanding of how the global economy affects the countries and people in Latin America. Individuals play the roles of various folks in a given country, such as farmers, factory workers, bankers, utility owners, and government officials. The leader of the game plays the role of the World Bank and the International Monetary Fund, the organizations that loan money to developing nations for high interest rates and according to tight guidelines. The game is a bit like Monopoly in that everyone starts out with a set amount of money and tries to make a go of it in the free market.

Basically, because of the high interest rates soon the rich get richer and the poor get poorer. The money that does not go into the pockets of corrupt politicians and business people is used to pay only the interest on the IMF and World Bank loans while the size of the basic debt itself never decreases. The guidelines require the governments to privatize all industry and this means the elimination of public services such as hospitals and schools. The local economy is limited to growing things like coffee, sugar, bananas, and rubber for export, leaving no time or space in which to grow food for local people. This is the price less privileged countries must pay in order to play in the global economy.

Once again, although no BorderLinks participants actually have much of anything to say about the operation of the global economy, this skit focuses the fact that the economies poorer nations are entirely dependent on those of the wealthier countries, like our own. Moreover, this skit makes it clear that the success of North American economies is in inverse proportion to those of oppressed nations. Here, too, we North Americans have an opportunity to see ourselves objectified as our commitments and behavior are acted out in the midst of this skit. Consciousness, as well as conscience can be and are raised by such exercises.

The application of the specific techniques devised by Paulo Freire for the education of the oppressed to the work of BorderLinks in the education of the oppressor is, to be sure, not straight forward. Yet it can be seen to be both possible and practical, especially when one is willing to invert these tactics so as to make them roughly fit the situation on the US/Mexico border. They can still embody the dynamics of a radical approach to the pedagogical enterprise. In the next chapter we shall turn to a more thorough look at some of the issues raised in this present discussion by the notions of generative themes and limit-situations. Freire has a great deal more to say about these concerns and it bears directly on the overall concern of developing a pedagogy of the oppressor.

Chapter Three

The Dimensions of Oppression

FREIRE'S CONCERN WITH EXPLORING the thematic universe of oppressed people has already been mentioned in the previous chapter. He sought to probe and make explicit the broad topics and issues that form the warp and weft of a given peoples' way of existing in the world where they find themselves. Freire termed these topics and issues generative themes and insisted that domination and development are the main themes in our own time.

In seeking to apply Freire's notion of the thematic universe to the task of educating people who are, however unwittingly, members of the oppressor or privileged class it is once again necessary to invert the direction or vector of Freire's analysis. For here we shall be dealing with the thematic universe of those who unwittingly by virtue of their economic and political practices and policies exploit and oppress others. The thematic universes of these two groups are quite different from each other, but are at the same time interconnected, since the one is largely caused by the other.

1. The First World Universe

The following consideration of the five themes that generate the universe within and according to which those of us living in the "First World" is by no means complete. It would not be difficult to suggest several additional themes comprising what Freire calls the generative fan of themes determining the assumptions and values governing the thought and behavior of the First World populations. Nonetheless, the five themes presented will at least be representative of and sufficient to provide an overview of the sort of factors that make up the fabric of life in the privileged world. The reader can think of others as well.

Once again something needs to be said about the difficulties of using such terms as 'first world' and 'third world,' 'developed/developing,' and the like. Not only is the use of such terms tiresome but none of them are very exact. Nonetheless, these are the terms that are usually used. Indeed, we are once again confronted here with the difficult task of naming reality with inevitably misleading words. I must beg the reader's indulgence as I try to alternate within this limited vocabulary.

We can begin with the theme of independence or freedom. In many ways this theme is perhaps the most important of all of those making up the universe of especially those of us living in North America. For, the United States of America was founded on the notions of independence and freedom, specifically in relation to the then repressive governments of Western Europe three hundred years ago. In addition, our Constitution guarantees us freedom of religion and keeps it separate from governmental control.

Even though it generally goes unstated, our commitment to individual freedom is part and parcel of the very air we breathe. We begin by assuming that we or anyone else can do or think whatever they like until a good reason is given as to why they cannot. We still hear the expression: "Why not? It's a free country." In addition, the Bill of Rights directly specifies certain individual rights that cannot in principle be denied any citizen. We also believe that all people ought to be free and independent in these ways, and we claim to be committed to helping them do so.

An important dimension of this fundamental belief in the independence and freedom of every person is a thorough going commitment to the philosophy of individualism. As noted earlier on, the basic Western belief that we all come into this world as separate individuals, as distinct atoms of reality, and that all of relationships beyond those of immediate family, are a function of choice, runs as deep as it goes far back in our history. Naturally, then, we project and embody this view onto other peoples as well, even though such individualism has not, until recently, been characteristic of Third World cultural beliefs.

A related theme, one that Freire might call a hinge theme, is that of control. A person who is independent and free is in control of his or her own life and destiny, even as the MasterCard slogan used to say: "Take control of the possibilities." We in the West are constantly being told not to let anyone control us, to look out for Number One, and to be all we can be. So it is that we in North America are inextricably entwined with the ideas of independence, freedom, and control.

When Freire sought to reveal their thematic universe to oppressed people, he did so by pointing the inherent contradictions in each aspect of their lives. Even while they would have embraced each of the foregoing themes for themselves, at the same time he pointed out that they were also committed to and lived lives which embraced basic commitments to family and community. They clearly valued co-operation and sought the common good. They would not in any way embrace the worlds extoled by the likes of Thomas Hobbes and Ayan Rand, in the name of absolute freedom and independence.

Finally, to turn to the issue of control, the fact of the matter is when controlling one's own life and options becomes the order, it is not long before we realize that to do so requires that we begin to control others, both economically and even militarily. This is why North American foreign policy, especially in Latin America, has for over a century been one of controlling the other nations, both economically and militarily, it was initially called "The Monroe Doctrine" by President Monroe. Individualistic notions of independence and freedom, then, cannot be affirmed by Third World peoples without giving rise to an inherent self-contradiction within this system.

A second theme comprising our Western and North American conceptual and behavioral universe is that of achievement or success. From our very birth into Western culture we are told that we can and must amount to something; that we can become whatever we want to be if we only try hard enough. It simply is not acceptable in our culture not to strive for ever more success and accomplishment regardless of the cost. In our culture no one is ever allowed to be content with what he or she has attained or obtained, even though we sometimes give lip-service to contentment and humility.

Especially in North America, what matters most in terms of personal identity and worth is what we have been able to accomplish, and what we plan to do next. Thus it is that we judge other societies by the same criterion and find them wanting. By and large, in Latin American countries people tend to identify and value persons in terms of their family connections and regional affiliations. We in North America, in our individualism, believe that each person can and should be a winner. Our advertisements are continually telling us to be winners in spite of the fact that logically speaking we cannot all be winners, since for every winner here must be at least one loser. Indeed, in nearly all contests everyone who is not the winner is by definition a loser.

To see how deep this drive for achievement runs in our culture, it is only necessary to reflect on the fact that one of the very worst things we can say about someone is that they are a loser. This criterion of value goes hand in hand with the drive to gain or acquire ever greater and bigger awards, prizes, and money. The mark of success in the West is what and how much one has been able to accumulate, and this fact focuses a basic contradiction within the theme of achievement, namely that since there exists a limited number or amount of resources, of any kind in the world, when one or a few persons accumulate a lot of them, other persons must go without. In a real, functional world resources must be shared.

It should not go unmentioned that in the West it is the advertisement world that largely plays the role that drawings and photos play in Freire's analysis of the behavioral patterns of the oppressed people. These advertisements portray of who we are and what we value. Indeed, money is almost always at the center of both our advertisements and our social values. As the saying goes, "You should be willing to put your money where your mouth is." Or as the ad says: "Don't leave home without it."

A third theme or pattern in the fabric of the North American thematic universe might be said to be that of industriousness and competition. Another one of the worst things one can say about another person in our culture is that he or she is lazy. Everyone is expected to work very hard at whatever it is they undertake, and each is expected to do better than others who do the same thing you do. The converse of this, and herein lies the contradiction, is that we generally conclude that a person who does not succeed must not be trying their best, they are, in fact, lazy. This is exactly the judgement that we frequently pass on people in the Third World, since they do not seem to prize industriousness as highly as we do. This explains the fact that their nations are "underdeveloped."

The competition aspect of this theme comes into play whenever people are challenged to excel at what they have chosen to do. They are challenged to get better at it, to become more and more industrious. For inevitably this will bring them into increased competition with others who are involved in the same enterprise. Youngsters compete to make the athletic team, and in so doing they must beat out the other youngsters for a spot on the team. Yet, they are all taught to develop team spirit, since once they are on a team they must work together. Another contradiction appears here, however, for they all want to have the same playing time, and thus this leads to continued competition, each individual against the others, but yet "all for one and one for all." And so it goes.

This same competitive pattern repeats itself throughout our lives, whether in school, at work, or in romance. We must always seek to do better and this brings us into competition with others who are doing likewise. A few will win, most will lose. Our commitment to individualism conflicts with the need for co-operation and commonality.

Our constant emphasis on winning and improving produces a great deal of stress in the lives of North Americans. Indeed, it can be said that we Americans work harder at our leisure than most other peoples do at their work. Herein lies yet another contradiction in the lives of North Americans. It is not acceptable in our culture for a person to say: "I am satisfied with who I am and with what I have." This does not even bring into account that terrific physical and mental toll this pattern takes on our psyches. As the song has it: "I'm another day older and deeper in debt."

Fourthly, North American culture is driven by a concern for comfort and convenience. Ours has been called the instant culture because we have come to desire all creature comforts and to expect them to be available now. The incredible flow of ever more gadgets to simplify and smooth out our lives is, in fact, almost unbelievable. "Technology is here to serve you!" has become our motto. Never run if you can walk, never walk if you can ride, never take the stairs if there is an elevator. A simple observation of North American impatience, at a traffic light, for instance, should be sufficient to make this aspect of our thematic universe clear.

As anyone who has traveled in the Third World knows, the pace there is slower and many of the conveniences we have come to take for granted are absent. In part this difference is a result of what we would call technological underdevelopment, but it also reflects a different value system in places where less of a premium is put on always seeking the easiest and quickest way of doing things. Here in North America one is suspect if he or she does not always seek the shortest way to a destination, does not always choose an upgrade, or allows others to go ahead in a checkout line.

This drive for comfort and convenience has led our society to consume and waste over three quarters of the world's resources even though we make up less than one quarter of the world's population. This has, in turn, driven us to exploit and oppress millions of people throughout the world in order to supply us with oil, sugar, coffee, rubber, bananas, and cheap labor in order to support us "in the style to which we have become accustomed." The Mexico/US border is a specific case in point here. The end result of the NAFTA policies has been to allow North American companies to locate their assembly plants just south of the border for low rent, no taxes, and cheap labor. The products and the money move north across the border, but the workers cannot move. It really should be called NAFLA, the North American Free Labor Agreement.

Finally, Western culture is characterized by a mania for the new, for progress. We have come to believe, at a very deep level, that whatever is old and traditional is basically worthless while whatever is new and innovating is of greater value. Even the reliable products in the marketplace cannot rest on their laurels, they must continually be updated with a fresh version of themselves. Tide detergent must be replaced by new and improved Tide. Classic Coke and classic Mustangs are always in need of newer models, so much so that it has become difficult if not impossible to see what they have in common with the older version.

In order to test out this claim just try to criticize something for being new or innovating in an everyday conversation. You will be met with blank confused stares. We in the West truly believe that today is inherently better than yesterday, and that tomorrow will even be better. In contrast, traditional Asian cultures viewed the other way around. For them whatever is old, or traditional, is clearly better and whatever is new is suspect. If one questions the reliability of this observation about our own culture, consider how we have come to worship youth and to denigrate old age. We have lost appreciation and respect for older persons in our society because we believe that the future will always be better. As General Electric used to put it: "Progress is our most important product."

It is time now to turn our attention to what BorderLinks, an organization that seeks to educate the oppressor class into seeing and acknowledging that we are, in fact, the oppressor, goes about its chosen task. The goal is to enable North Americans to confront, in a transformative way, our own worldview, our own thematic universe so that we can better comprehend the reality faced by the Third World peoples and to thereby be in a position to do something about the situation. Throughout its more than three decade history BorderLinks has developed various techniques by means of which it endeavors to raise the consciousness and consciences of North American peoples and some of these techniques are worthy of mention here.

The main means at BorderLinks disposal is, of course, simply bringing North Americans to the border region, and arranging for them to encounter the realities there, as well as to be able to interact with the people living and working there. This experiential encounter not only serves to inform these visitors about the conditions along the border, but it works as a mirror of our own culture as well. That is to say, by interacting with folks along the border, we North Americans come to see and understand our own thematic universe in an entirely fresh way. This alone can trigger a rise of consciousness and conscience.

In addition, the different simulation games that BorderLinks staff members play with the visitors involving role-playing provide an excellent opportunity for these delegates to become aware of the various economic and political patterns at work in today's global economy and to discern the part we in the US play in making things happen to our own advantage. Again, we are thereby enabled to see ourselves objectified once again.

Another experiential aspect of this process of raising North American consciousness and conscience gets focused by calling attention to the numerous media messages to which Mexican families are exposed. Newspapers, radios, and especially television all carry a decidedly North American flavor or spin and frequently we North Americans can thereby see ourselves and our value system blatantly displayed in the way products and programs are presented. As was noted earlier on, one's student's deep embarrassment over the ad for *White Magic* skin cream is a powerful case in point.

In the Culture of the Borderlands course offered in BorderLinks' semester on the border program there are many occasions when it is profitable to step back from our own media and consider the sub-text involved in what is presented and how it is presented. The obvious, but largely unnoticed contrast, for instance, between the joyful ads that surround magazine and newspaper articles about terrible events or situations around the world is an indictment of our culture. The same contrast can be seen between the news on television and the upbeat ads that follow and precede it.

We skip over ever so lightly from deep devastation to business as usual, to ads for tires, cars, snappy clothes, and expensive jewelry, never stopping to ask how our feeling of entitlement to these luxuries helps bring about many of the oppressive conditions in the Third World. People are not poor by accident, and it is a real eye-opener for North Americans to have their own thematic universe displayed to them in such dramatic fashion. The process of observing and reviewing the media presentation of our own culture is not unlike that employed by Freire in working with oppressed folks, but here it is the oppressors who see themselves afresh.

By far the most effective means of helping us North Americans get a better grasp of our own worldview and value system is that of simply returning from the border to our regular places of work and living. Scores of BorderLinks participants have made it clear, year in and year out, that the biggest culture shock for them was returning home. They are then forced to see what they truly value and ask about why things must be this way. The sweet ads for the Columbian coffee grown by friendly Juan no longer go unnoticed and unquestioned. Nor does the enormous tonnage of wasted food and other resources that we North Americans take for granted.

A very frequent observation made by BorderLinks visitors to the border has to do with the fact that the people with whom they interacted, especially on the Mexican side, are not free to move in order to improve their situation, while we North Americans can simply go home when we grow tired of the difficult conditions we face while visiting there. The incredible freedom that we enjoy in being able to go to the border to experience first-hand the conditions and people there, and then simply pick up and go back to the comforts of home, generally goes unnoticed and unappreciated.

Once this freedom is brought to consciousness and its implications begin to sink in, a wedge is driven into the oppressors' mindset that just may allow for a truly transformative experience in the conscience of a member of the privileged class. The pedagogy of the oppressor may actually have begun.

2. Decoding Themes

In Freire's approach to the pedagogy of the oppressed, once the thematic universe has been identified and explored the focus shifts to the process of "decoding" the individual themes. By this term Freire means finding specific examples of or embodiments of the themes in the everyday lives of those people in question and eliciting an awareness and analysis of them from the people themselves. Such recognition actually constitutes the first phase of the consciousness raising experience. Here he and his helpers used photos and drawings of everyday life in village or *colonia* life by way of showing the people to themselves.

One such example has already been mentioned, namely that in which the laborers recognized one of their compadres both as a drunk and as one of them. On another occasion there was a drawing of the village men working in the fields while yet another man leans on a shovel. When asked "What is that man doing?" the workers involved on the exercise replied that he is the foreman, the *jefe,* who makes sure that they all do their work. When asked how hard the foreman works, the men reply that he has an easy job. But when asked how well the foreman gets paid, they answer that he makes much more than they themselves do.

Generally at this point a discussion ensues about why things are this way and what might be done about this disparity. The workers become aware that even though the foreman is one of them, he also represents the owner's interest and advantage. The workers admit that they are both proud of their foreman and bitter towards him because he "lords it over" them. Also, as one of the paradoxes of oppression, the workers envy the foreman and hope that someday they will be chosen for this position by the *patron.*

As has been made clear all along, Freire insists that at every step of this educative process the mode of communication is that of interactive dialogue, not unilateral monologue. The teachers or leaders must always approach those with whom they work at their own level and they must use a question/answer format. As he puts it: "The program content of the problem-posing method—dialogical par-excellence—is constituted and organized by the students' view of the world, where their own generative themes are found. The content then constantly expands and renews itself. The task of the dialogical teacher in an interdisciplinary working on a thematic universe by their investigation is to re-present that universe to the people from whom he first received it—and 're-present' it not as a lecture but as a problem."[1]

As was noted earlier on, this dialogical interaction cannot be carried out apart from the incorporation of love, faith, trust, and hope. Authentic communication can only occur in the context of honest listening and openness to growth. Sometimes, according to Freire, so-called "revolutionary leaders" forget this fundamental fact and seek to force their own agenda onto the people from the top down. The real task of true pedagogy is to arrange the context and carry on the discussion in such a way as to promote genuine insight and transformation.

The actual concrete dynamics of the decoding process, whether conducted with the oppressed or the oppressors is an interactive one in which both the teacher and the student progress in back-and-forth exchanges

1. Freire, *Pedagogy,* 109.

from a specific instance of a particular cultural theme to the abstract notion of which the instance is but an expression. Freire focuses the issue in the following way: "This dialectical movement of thought is exemplified perfectly in the analysis of a concrete, existential, 'coded' situation. Its decoding requires moving from the abstract to the concrete; this requires moving from the part to the whole and then returning to the parts; this in turn requires that the Subject recognizes himself in the object (the coded concrete existential situation) and recognizes the object as a situation in which he finds himself, together with other Subjects."[2]

One cannot help but being reminded of pedagogical method employed by Socrates in ancient Athens. Down through history this method has been labelled the Socratic method or simply the dialogical method of education. The crucial assumption undergirding this approach is that together the teacher and the learner can and will come to a genuine understanding of the issue at hand, will draw out the knowledge needed and sought. It should be noted that this interpretation of the Greek term for educate, or educe, as a process of mutual interaction and discovery, differs from the more traditional interpretation of the term 'educate,' which maintains that what is to be known or learned, is already within the learner's mind and only needs to be drawn out.

Although the above referenced difference might at first seem esoteric and academic, a deeper consideration of it makes its cruciality quite clear. For, in Freire's understanding of how knowledge comes about the dialogue between the teacher and the learner is an authentic one in which they arrive at it *together,* while in the traditional interpretation of Socrates' view the knowledge is already present in the mind of the learner and only needs to be drawn out. Thus in the latter case the dialogue is only a throw away technique for drawing out what is already present. It is open to debate whether Socrates himself actually thought he was "educing" already present knowledge from the mind of the learner, or whether he, like Freire, really believed that together he and his learners could eventually arrive at the truth which was as yet not yet known to either of them.

In the previous chapter Freire was quoted as insisting on using examples for decoding that are neither too explicit nor too enigmatic. In the former case the danger is that dialogue is reduced to mere propaganda, while in the latter case it turns into a guessing game. In that context he went on to say: "Since they represent existential situations, the codifications should be

2. Freire, *Pedagogy*, 105.

simple in their complexity and offer various decoding possibilities in order to avoid the brain-washing tendencies of propaganda. Codifications are not slogans, they are cognizable objects, challenges towards which the critical reflection of the decoders should be directed."[3]

This same criteria must be invoked when considering the pedagogy of the oppressors as well. Once again, although the process is essentially the same in regards to the education of both the oppressed and the oppressors, the latter needs to be inverted so as to draw attention to the thematic universe of the privileged class or societies. Here, too, both brain-washing and guessing games need to be avoided. The interaction must be both honest and reflective.

The decoding process when applied to the educational task confronting BorderLinks might involve some of the following ways of proceeding, some of which have been touched already. In keeping with the activities suggested in the previous section, much of what can be done to help reveal their thematic universe to North Americans may well center around the analysis of the media, especially television. This approach works rather well in connection with the semester program since it provides more time and opportunity for extended reflection and discussion.

Take, for example, a television ad that appeared a few years back involving Pete Rose, a famous baseball player. It would not be difficult to find parallel examples among contemporary TV advertisements. This particular ad was for a men's after shave *Skin Bracer* and the final line was "A man wants to smell like a man." Aside from all the other issues involved, the underlying yet unspoken assumption is that there is a certain way men are supposed to smell and this differs markedly from the way women are supposed to smell. When first asked to "decode" this ad, many if not most North Americans fail to see anything beyond the implication that men should buy this after shave if they want to smell as men are supposed to smell, especially if they wish to be attractive to women. The fact that someone somewhere on Madison Avenue has determined that all men should smell the same, and is here claiming that this particular product will make men smell that way, goes pretty much unnoticed. We take it for granted that there is a way men are supposed to smell and that we should conform to this behavior.

By sharing this ad with the BorderLinks' participants one can surface an awareness of the extent to which our society is shaped by those people

3. Freire, *Pedagogy*, 115.

who want to sell products, even down to how we should smell. The marketplace largely determines our values, since advertising agencies create the desire for certain products quite apart from whether or not the public asks for them. Ours is a supply side economy in which what the public demands is largely determined by those who make products for us to consume and then persuade us to buy them.

Another dimension of our culture, of our thematic universe, embedded in ads like this one is that the way men and women are supposed to smell—or look, or act, etc.—is a predetermined matter and not subject to alternative definitions. Moreover, to look more deeply, it is generally men who determine such things, since it is very largely men who run major companies and advertising agencies. It has become acceptable for women to wear traditionally male clothes, such as pants, and even boxer shorts. But one wonders if men will ever be free to wear skirts and high heeled shoes. Ours is a highly conformist culture despite all the rhetoric about everyone being free to choose to become whoever and whatever they want to be.

It is, of course, but a short step from realizing that our society is largely run by the marketplace to coming to see that this same dynamic is what governs the international economy as well. The Third World countries are told how they should behave, what they should produce and consume, and we North Americans do most of the telling. Whatever we want, Third World countries produce, such as drugs, petroleum, and weapons, even if they themselves would never think of using the products they make for us. It should be part of our own decoding process that enables us to see and appreciate such strange paradoxes.

The advertising world is constantly telling us to look, eat, and behave like this or that not because we chose to, but because there are products it wishes to sell. In so doing it plays upon our emotions ("Chevy, like a rock"), our guilt "(What happens to your loved ones when you die?"), and our aspirations ("Be all you can be!"). Even some vending machines in public restrooms provide a mirror and motherly advice ("Don't neglect your appearance!"). Unfortunately, people in the Third World are also subjected to this type of advertising, mostly ours, but they have very few resources with which to participate in its manufactured game, supply and demand. In spite of this, or because of it, they are sucked into believing that the more products a person possesses the better and happier he or she will be. Consider the Pantene ad: "Full bodied hair builds a full-bodied soul."

Another opportunity for BorderLinks to help North Americans decode their own thematic universe is provided by the issue of recycling plastic, paper, and cardboard items. It is extremely surprising as well as disappointing, to see how little effort and understanding there is among North Americans concerning the amount of pollution we are producing on this planet. Just the simple task of educating BorderLinks participants as to how to collect, fold, and flatten recyclable items can be an eye-opening experience. To actually place a recycling bin and a trashcan in the midst of border visitors and ask them to discuss the difference between them is often quite an educational experience.

The simple fact is that we are a "throw-away" society. We are so used to everything being convenient and replaceable that it almost never occurs to us to think about the consequences of what we do with our various types of packaging containers. It is particularly interesting to see how North Americans react to the trash, junk, and disposables that characterize many Third World towns and villages, to say nothing of big cities. The only real difference between their environment and ours is that we pay people to collect our garbage and hide it in landfills. Ultimately most of it is either buried or floating on the oceans. "Out of sight, out of mind" is our motto.

Hopefully it becomes clear just how these sorts of decoding opportunities can serve to open up the various generative themes comprising the North American worldview. All of the themes mentioned in the previous section of this chapter are illustrated in the examples taken up in this section. Our deep belief in entitlement to freedom and individual independence gives us license to consume whatever and as much as we wish. Our commitment to success and achievement allows us to control and exploit economic markets and Third World peoples with little concern for other peoples' wellbeing. Indeed, in a real sense our abilities to waste, pollute and control serve as our symbols of our affluence, industry, and superiority.

The most important point to remember in this review of our own cultural themes is that not only do many aspects of our way of life as privileged (over-privileged?) wreak havoc on the people of the Third World countries, but it places us in what Freire calls *limit-situations*, contexts that have extremely detrimental effects on our individual and corporate lives. At the deepest possible level the thematic universe in which we as the ruling class have come to exist is a prison of the worst possible kind because it belies the fact that in exploiting and oppressing others one cannot help but to do so to one's self as well. To be an oppressor is to be oppressed.

3. Limit Situations

Freire defines a limit-situation as resulting from the generative themes making up a people's worldview or thematic universe. They are the concrete manifestations of the over-arching framework within which a culture or society is encountered in the everyday life of the people. They are, in Freire's words "the concrete historical dimensions of a given reality."[4] He goes on to say that everything depends on whether these limits are seen as fetters that can be broken or as insurmountable barriers that cannot.

When working with oppressed people the central challenge is to enable them to treat their self-limitations as fetters rather than as insurmountable barriers, since the former can be broken or released, but the latter cannot. Oppressed people tend to think of their limit situations as set for life and of themselves as powerless to alter them. A dialogical pedagogy of liberation aims at transforming these understandings through an interactive analysis of various limit-situations which seek to trace them back to the generative themes that they make concrete.

It is important not to interpret Freire's notion of limit-situations in metaphysical or theological terms, thereby suggesting that they reflect certain aspects of human nature per se. This is the mistake, for example, Dennis McCann makes in his influential *Christian Realism and Liberation Theology*. In contrasting Freire's thought to that of theologian Reinhold Niebuhr, McCann focuses on this idea of limits and complains that for Freire there are only historical and social limitations, no ontologial ones that define the human condition as such. Niebuhr on the other hand, according to Mc-Cann, is more realistic in stressing the limitations that characterize what it means to be a human finite creature.[5]

The difficulty here, and where McCann goes wrong, is in failing to see that Freire is not addressing the human condition in general with his concept of limit-situations. Rather, he is speaking directly to the specific historical, social, and politico-economic conditions that arise as a result of the worldview or thematic universe within which a given people live as the result of the realities they confront.

The simple fact is that one cannot infer from Freire's treatment of limit-situations as historical, socio-political, economic phenomena that he has no place in his thought for broader, more metaphysical categories. The

---

4. Freire, *Pedagogy*, 99.

5. McCann, *Christian Realism*, 172–75.

book *Pedagogy of the Oppressed* is not a theological or metaphysical study, but rather presents a philosophy of education for a specific time and place. Freire in no way implies that human beings are not finite creatures with certain limitations, etc. as regards to what they can or cannot accomplish. Thus the contrast with Niebuhr's analysis of human nature is quite out of place in McCann's comparison of liberation theology and christian realism.

Freire is primarily concerned with enabling oppressed people to understand their concrete situation and how to take action so as to transform it. Although there may well be limits to what such people can accomplish as finite created beings, it remains true that there is much that they can accomplish within such broader limitations. It is these specific tasks that Freire is addesssing when he speaks of limit-situations. We shall return to this broader question of what he thinks about human nature in the next section.

Limit-situations, then, for Freire's purposes are created by the confluence of events and concerns which press in on a given group of people as a result of the worldview within which they live, and as such they in one way or another dehumanize these people. Oppressed people must come to see these limitations as temporary blocks to their own fulfillment, blocks about which it is possible to do something transformative.

When it comes to discussing the limit-situations which characterize the world-view or thematic universe of the ruling class, the oppressors, things get a bit more complicated. Once again it is necessary to invert Freire's categories and methods somewhat in order to make them applicable to the privileged folks of North America. The same format still works, but the content of the limit-situations confronting oppressors is different. Indeed, at first glance it may seem to make little sense to speak of the privileged class as having limiting situations at all, but a second look is in order here.

The fact of the matter is that this is precisely where the task of educating the oppressor class becomes both significant and difficult. For, whereas oppressed people may readily admit that they exist within limiting situations, both they and their oppressors have a most difficult time admitting that the latter too exist within limiting situations. Whereas with the oppressed the goal is to help them see that there is something they can do about their readily admitted socio-political limitations, with the oppressors the goal is to get them to acknowledge that they have any limit-situations in the first place.

Indeed, one of the more forceful generative themes making up the North American conceptual and behavioral universe is that of individual freedom and choice. Our whole culture literaly screams at us that we are absolutely free to be whatever we choose to be. The only limitations we have, it would seem, are those that we set for ourselves. We do and like to think of ourselves as Johathan Livingston Seagull, free to soar above every situation that would bind or limit us. How can the oppressors be limited?

So, not only do members of the oppressor class think it is a negative thing to have any limitations, we generally refuse to acknowledge that we ourselves might, in fact, have any. This then becomes the challenge facing those, like BorderLinks, who seek to educate the oppressors concerning their own limit-situations. To raise consciousness, as well as well as conscience, about one's own acknowledged predicament is a Herculean task, indeed. Or perhaps to call it a Socratic task would be more appropriate since Socrates claimed that the first and necessary step in acquiring knowledge is to be willing to admit that one does not possess it already.

The crucial thing to understand here is that we are not speaking of limitations in the usual sense when we speak of the limit-situations besetting the oppressor class. Rather, we are designating as limiting situations precisely those qualities and traits which are generally thought of as strengths. The claim here is that it is the very characteristics which most folks see as strengths, such as our belief in individual freedom, success, industry, convenience, and progress, that have and are actually imprisoning us as North Americans. Our limit-situations are the backside of what we regard as our strengths.

To put it differently, the values of our thematic universe frequently implode on themselves because they are pursued in narrow and shortsighted ways, ways that dehumanize us and in turn dehumanize others through exploitation and oppression. Thus, the oppressor class is, infact, itself oppressed by its own value system. To put it another way, the oppressors are also oppressed and along with the oppressed stand in need of liberation.

The crucial fact to keep in mind when attempting to draw oppressors' attention to the limitations or downside inherent within the very value system that they themselves think is their own core strength is that this can only be accomplished indirectly. That is to say, very little if any progress can be made by way of direct confrontation. Here again a reference to the Socratic pedagogical method seems appropriate. Even though it is generally safe to say that Socrates knew more than his students about the topic at hand, he always engaged them in a dialogical process which focused on the pressing issue or idea rather than lecturing or arguing with them.

Even as Freire's work clearly illustrates, it is by seeing themselves objectified, as it were, in their own lives that oppressed people are able to grasp their limit-situations, along with the broader generative themes which create them. This is no less true when one is dealing with oppressors as themselves oppressed people. Direct conflict or lecturing only results in defensiveness at worst and a guilt complex at best. Neither of these results is conducive to genuine consiousness raising and transformation.

As has been pointed out all along, the BorderLinks way of working towards these goals is deliberately indirect in that it seeks to place the learner squarely in the midst of a living context with concrete persons and to use questions and discussion by way of exploring local conditions, possible causes and solutions. So too, when seeking to raise the consciousness and conscience of the oppressive and privileged class concerning its own type of self-oppression, the same indirect approach is applicable.

This sort of indirect approach is most effectively fostered by experiential education, namely by actually engaging with other persons and actually encountering their living and working conditions. This is an indirect approach in that it stresses contact and interaction while avoiding lecturing and sermonizing. To actually be in a real situation, experiencing what people on the border experience, if only briefly, is worth a ton of lectures. BorderLinks strives to create and facilitate such experiences as the way to gain genuine understanding.

One exercise that helps focus a limit-situation of North Americans is that of noting just how many things we think we are unable to do without. Just the sheer number of bags and clothes, to say nothing of credit cards, cell phones, and laptops that we consider necessary can be astonishing. Almost every visitor to the border brings along more stuff and devices than the average Mexican citizen could ever hope to own. Many such visitors are deeply struck by this comparison and engage in a good deal of self-examination and discussion over it.

The extremely limiting character of our lifestyle should be obvious. As Henry David Thoreau put it well before our culture was overtaken by the illness known as "affluenza": "We all stagger along the road weighed down by the heavy mortgage on our back." Our credit card debt disease alone is highly indicative of this particular limit-situation, and one is made vividly aware of how dehumanizing being overly affluent can be.

On one of the semester program trips the students got to visit Mata Ortiz, a small village of about three hundred people in Chihuahua, Mexico.

The story of this village is remarkable and well-known. A number of years ago a young man named Juan Quesada found some old potsherds left over from a nearby ancient ruin and taught himself to make copies of them. Soon he was making shapes and designs of his own and became a very accomplished potter. Juan taught his brother to be a potter and together they taught the rest of the family and some neighbors this skill. Before long the entire village was full of excellent potters and has in fact become internationally famous.

When discussing this phenomenon the students were very impressed by two things. First, Juan Quesada shared his new-found skill with anyone who was interested. He did not hide his techniques from the competition and as a result all of the people benefitted. This reminded the students of the *ejido* co-operative farms that used to thrive throughout Mexico before they were eliminated by NAFTA in the name of privatization. The students were struck by our North American need to compete rather than co-operate with one another. They saw it as a limit-situation for the over privileged oppressors.

Second, the students soon realized that this village had found a way to make their lives viable economically and so to avoid having to migrate north in order to make ends meet. Almost all of the people living in the border region have migrated from small towns and villages in central Mexico in order to find work. The people of Mata Ortiz have been fortunate, and this caused the students to wish other villages could find some way to make a living in their original home.

The limiting character of the problem highlighted by the need to migrate and end up working in a factory was mirrored for the students in our own work-a-day world where nearly all of us work for someone else at jobs we often only tolerate. The economic system of capitalism, which we have come to take for granted, thrives on competition and essentially selling oneself to the highest bidder. Most folks in the First World live their lives looking forward to weekends, vacations, and retirement without really being able to follow their own dreams. This is clearly a limiting situation.

On a somewhat different note, one of the BorderLinks staff members volunteered to play Santa Claus at the Casa Misericordia Christmas party for nearly thousand children. It was an eye-opening experience to say the least. The first year the children filed by Santa with blank stares, keeping their distance. He tried to joke with them and shake their hands, but with little success. It was obvious that although they knew who Santa is, he was not part of their experience of Christmas. In fact, most of them had never seen Santa except in pictures or on TV.

The second year, things were very different. At the *Posada*, a drama portraying the Christmas story, Santa was introduced and asked to distribute candy to the children. This he did with some gusto, tossing Tootsie Rolls to the children over his head, behind his back, and through his legs. The kids were very enthusiastic. Next, Santa was asked to dance, and so he spun down the aisle doing his rendition of the Mexican Hat Dance. The children went berserk. Santa was now a part of the celebration and was accepted.

This time when the children filed past Santa to receive their gifts they were all smiles and full of laughter. They sat on his lap and poked his much too large stomach. The staff member in question could not help but contrast this whole event with the few times he had been Santa at his own church Christmas party. There the kids were either bored by Santa or only interested in getting the candy canes he gave out, to which they felt fully entitled. At the same time, it would have been disrespectful for Santa to dance at the church Christmas party, for such behavior would break the spell surrounding the small children's belief in him.

This experience calls attention to the two-faced nature of the entire Santa Claus phenomenon in North America. One the one hand, his reality is surrounded by an almost religious aura, while on the other hand he is an essentially commercial entity who symbolizes the total materialism to which North Americans have succumbed. He cannot deviate from either of these roles. The encounter with Mexican Santa fulfilled neither of these functions. He was free to dance and distribute gifts playfully without fear of disturbing some child's belief in the divinity of Santa Claus.

For this staff member, as well as for other staff members, these contrasting experiences were a revelation of the limit-situations surrounding the way most North Americans think of our most significant holidays as well as of other cultural figures. Not only do we tend to reduce all celebrations to a commercial or media event, but at the same time we also seek to endow them with a mystique that overly controls our behavior. The billions of dollars spent on Christmas gifts frequently out of some sense of obligation created by the advertising agencies bears witness to the stultifying character of this form of self-oppression.

Perhaps the most powerful aspect of this staff member's consciousness raising in connection with this experience of playing Santa was the degree to which North American children expect, even take for granted, all the gifts involved in Christmas, even down to the way some kids often grab candy from Santa's hands, or try to get more than their share of the gifts he passes out. The sense of entitlement seems, sadly, to be behind a great many of North American attitudes and behaviors.

The Mexican children, by contrast, never seemed overly concerned about how much candy or how many gifts they received from Santa. They accepted what they were given without acting as if they were entitled to any of it. Thus, although Third World children are clearly limited in material advantages, it is even more clear that First World children are often limited by the degree to which they have come to expect that they should have more than their fair share of whatever is available. As Sally used to say in the Peanuts cartoons "I want to be sure that I get my fair share." It should be obvious that such an attitude is extremely dehumanizing and limiting to First World and Third World people alike.

This philosophy of entitlement seems to run throughout the North American value system and its diverse cultural expressions. We North Americans have come to believe that we are the best in everything, that we are and must be "Number One" in every endeavor. From the Gross National Product index to scientific and technological discoveries, to athletic competitions we are taught to assume that we have earned the right to be first. The limiting character of such arrogance should be self-evident.

It is important not to allow an awareness of such limit-situations to give rise to pessimism or cynicism. As Freire continually reminded the oppressed peoples with whom he worked, everything depends on whether we see limit-situations as fetters that can be broken or removed, or as insurmountable barriers which lock a people into their own worldview. These limit-situations embodying the thematic universe of North Americans are not written in stone, but are amenable to reform and reconstruction. There have been activist movements throughout history which have brought about genuine change and improvement in the world even if they have not brought about utopia.

From the signing of the Magna Charta and the Protestant Reformation, through the movements ignited by Mahatma Gandhi and Martin Luther King, Jr. to Nelson Mandela and recent political turnarounds in Europe and Latin America it is possible to see positive transformations among the peoples of our world. The very purpose of the BorderLinks vision and program is founded on the belief that people and nations can change for the better through educational experience involving interactive dialogue and direct encounter between and among those who are committed to genuine transformation. Such progress does not come about on its own. The road to transformation is made by walking.

4. The Human Animal

Before moving on to an examination of the final phases of Freire's presentation of the pedagogy of the oppressed, it is worthwhile to consider his own excursion into the question of human nature. In the midst of his analysis of the concepts generative themes and limit-situations, Freire spends several pages reflecting on the difference between the human animal and other animals. His overall purpose in doing so is to focus ever more forcefully the crucial role of self-transcendence and free choice in the existence of human beings as distinguished from other animal life forms.

Apparently drawing on the insights of John Paul Sartre's work *Existentialism Is A Humanism*, Freire argues that whereas nonhuman animals exist concretely "in-themselves" in a sort of flat unilateral form of life, humans exist historically "for-themselves" in a self-reflective way that enables them to be self-conscious about their own decisions and behavior even as they engage in them. Freire expresses his point this way: "Because the animals' activity is an extension of themselves, the results of their activity are also inseparable from themselves. Animals can neither set objectives nor infuse their transformation with any significance beyond itself. Moreover, the 'decision' to perform this activity belongs not to them but to their species. Animals are, accordingly, fundamentally 'beings in themselves.'"[6]

Freire goes on to illustrate his point by showing how animals, unlike humans, are incapable of exhibiting behavior which involves historical concepts such as here, now, tomorrow, and yesterday. Their life is almost entirely in the present, with only the immediate future in view. One can, for instance, inform a dog that Harry is coming or that we shall go for a walk, but not that Harry is coming next week, or that we shall go for a walk tomorrow.

> Unable to decide for themselves, unable to objectify either themselves or their activity, lacking objectives which they themselves have set, living 'submerged' in a world to which they can give no meaning, lacking a 'tomorrow' and a 'today' because they exist in an overwhelming present, animals are ahistorical . . . Humans, however, because they are aware of themselves and thus of the

6. Freire, *Pedagogy*, 97.

world—because they are conscious beings—exist in a dialectical relationship between the determination of limits and their own freedom. As they separate themselves from the world, which they objectify, as they separate themselves from their own activity, as they locate the seat of their decisions in themselves and in their relations with the world and others, people overcome the situations which limit them: their 'limit situations.'[7]

Freire puts this point somewhat differently, drawing on Karl Marx's *Economic and Philosophical Manuscripts*, when he focuses on the difference between animals and humans with regard to the things they make. "Thus when animals 'produce' a nest, a hive, or a burrow, they are not creating products which result from 'limit acts,' that is transforming responses. Their productive activity is subordinated to the satisfaction of a physical necessity, which is stimulating rather than challenging. 'An animal's product belongs immediately to his physical body, whilst man freely confronts his product.'"[8]

To be sure, it may be questionable whether or not Freire, or even Marx, has drawn this distinction between animals and humans carefully enough. In recent years a great deal of information has been gathered about the behavior, and especially the decision making processes of the more complex creatures in the animal world. It now seems that line between animals and humans is much thinner than has traditionally been thought. Perhaps these two life forms should be thought of as existing on a continuum rather than as being essentially distinct.

Nevertheless, Freire's overall point remains well taken. It is clearly the case that the human animal participates in what phenomenological thinkers, such as Edmund Husserl and Maurice Merleau-Ponty, refer to as "intentionality." That is to say, humans project their awareness and behavior forward into projects and goal-directed activity. In brief, they are said to have a will or decision making capacity by means of which they can alter their world.

This is the reason Freire spends several pages exploring this issue. It clearly impinges on his concern to make the point that humans are capable of choosing to interact with their world, of altering and even transforming it into something more conducive to human good. In short, Freire contends that when confronted with limit-situations humans can engage in what he

7. Freire, *Pedagogy*, 98–99.
8. Freire, *Pedagogy*, 100.

calls "limit-acts" that interpret and respond to the debilitating conditions within which they find themselves.

As has already been mentioned, Freire insists that the crucial issue which arises when people become consciously aware of their limit-situations has to do with how they interpret them. On the one hand, they can see them as historical conditions that are susceptible to being altered through thought and action, through praxis. On the other hand, they can be viewed as impenetrable obstacles that forcefully define the simple realities of life and must be accepted as such. In the former case Freire says the limit- situations are seen as mere fetters, while in the latter case they are viewed as insurmountable barriers.

"As critical perception is embodied in action, a climate of hope and confidence develops which leads men (sic) to overcome the limit-situations. This objective can only be achieved through action upon the concrete historical reality in which the limit-situations are historically found. As reality is transformed and these situations are superseded, new ones will appear which in turn will evoke new limit-acts."[9]

The crucial factor in such transformations is, of course, the role of praxis. As Freire says: "Only human beings *are* praxis—the praxis, which as the reflection and action which truly transform reality, is the source of knowledge and creation."[10] It is also important to understand that Freire sees human action as actually creating reality, including material objects, but also social realities which include political, social, economic, and religious institutions, concepts and aspirations, as well as history and plans for the future. This reality takes the form of a "thematic universe" which defines a given culture.

When seeking to apply Freire's analysis of the oppressors' world it becomes necessary to once again stress that whatever appears to be an advantage within the thematic universe of the privileged may, in fact, be a limitation. The characteristics of a culture created by a privileged and ruling class are not only largely at the expense of an oppressed class, but often are in reality detrimental to the oppressor class itself. Thus oppressors are often confronted by limit-situations every bit as dehumanizing as those encountered by the oppressed, but at a far more subtle and debilitating level.

The deep and fundamental danger accompanying the limit-situations of the oppressor class is, indeed, their subtlety. For, as we argued in the

9. Freire, *Pedagogy*, 99–100.

10. Freire, *Pedagogy*, 100.

previous section, these limit-situations almost always appear to be advantages to those who live by them. Such is the paradoxical and insidious character of the reality plaguing the oppressive class in any society. Thus to engage in seeking to raise the consciousness of folks who are entirely or at least largely unaware of their limit-situations is as difficult as it is important. In order to deal with these limit-situations it is necessary to resort to what Freire calls a "de-coding" process.

The main consideration to bear in mind when approaching the task of consciousness raising with members of the ruling or privileged class is that they are by and large not conscious that they are in fact oppressing anyone. Moreover, in seeking to point out the oppressive character of their way of life in relation to the people of another country it is to be expected that they will become defensive and/or extremely guilt-ridden. The most difficult part of this endeavor, however, is to help such folks realize that their way of life and value system is, in fact, dehumanizing and debilitating to themselves.

After all, the idea of being Number One in nearly all respects would seem self-evidently valuable to a person conditioned to think of individual freedom, power, and success as necessary goods. The same holds true for the commitment to competitiveness and, industriousness, comfort, and convenience, as well as the belief in progress. To enable a person persuaded of the truth of such commitments to come to see their limitations and possible detrimental effect on themselves as well as others can be as frustrating as it is challenging.

Perhaps the first thing that can be said about how BorderLinks approaches this aspect of its task is that serious efforts are made to avoid trying to preach to those persons participating in various BorderLinks programs. As has been mentioned repeatedly, the BorderLinks staff seeks to create an arena within which an awareness of the true nature of the North American worldview will reveal itself to the participants as they participate in the program.

One concrete way this may be accomplished is by politely refusing to answer questions raised by participants in orientation sessions prior to the beginning of any given trip. Usually a simple remark, such as "Why don't you hold on to that query until we actually get to the border where you can see for yourself," will suffice. Likewise, when questions come up as the excursion progresses it helps to ask the participants to put their inquiry to the local people themselves, be they border patrol agents, *maquiladora* workers or managers, members of a squatter community, or migrants seeking to cross the border.

By redirecting questions back to the border residents themselves BorderLinks encourages the participants to observe more closely and actively reflect on their experiences without direct input or pressure from those facilitating their education. Very often the question will answer itself along the way or get answered directly by an appropriate border resident. If a participant still wishes to pursue the question at a later time, it can be taken up in the context of group discussion where all members of the delegation can pool their experiences and reflections. Such dialogue gives rise to genuine transformation in the minds and hearts of those involved.

As Freire points out repeatedly, it is crucial to enable those with whom one is working to see the difference between limit-situations as fetters and as insurmountable barriers. Sometimes when border visitors begin to realize the seriously negative aspects of their own worldview they feel paralyzed and incapable of doing anything about them. They see them as conditions which are impossible to do anything about. At such points it usually proves helpful to ask the other group members to brainstorm together about what sorts of ideas and projects might be workable to transform the situation in question. In this way the facilitator avoids lecturing, but at the same time generates the sort of dialogical interaction Freire recommends.

In a more structured classroom setting, as for instance with the semester program, it is also possible to redirect various questions by focusing on the particular text out of which the question arose. Here again one can create a dialogical arena for genuine interaction by incorporating the text's author as a participant in the conversation. Thus a triangle between the text, the questioner, and the rest of the group both disperses and intensifies the dialogue, thereby enhancing the possibility of real decision making on the part of the participants.

Another way to structure the learning context so as to maximize the activity of the decision making capacity of the members of the oppressor class is to challenge them to view their own worldview much as an anthropologist from Mars might view it. Stepping outside of one's own culture and mind-set and then viewing them as one among many others is every bit as valuable as it may prove difficult. Nevertheless, there is a great deal to be learned from just attempting this exercise because one is stretched significantly thereby. Anything that enables a person to objectify and reflect on their own way of being in the world has the potential to trigger consciousness raising experiences.

In conclusion it will be well to return to an emphasis that was introduced near the outset of this entire study. The real vision behind the BorderLinks operation is that it is by bringing North Americans into direct contact with folks living and working on the US/Mexico border that one hopes to see a transformative raising of consciousness in their lives. This is the genius of what is called experiential education in the BorderLinks promotional materials and the subtitle of this book.

Not only does experiential education provide the real content of any significant pedagogical endeavor, contrary to the traditional "banking" approach, but it does so in a way that allows for and even enhances the individual and collective observation and reflection necessary to the meaningful use of the human decision making capacity. This approach to education both stimulates learning on the part of those who participate in it while at the same time allowing them the necessary cognitive and emotional space within which to exercise their own reflective powers in dialogue with other members of their community.

Even the organizational procedures and processes in the BorderLinks enterprise are set up to follow this approach to decision making and human development. Both staff meetings and board meetings are conducted in an open and consensual manner, with every individual encouraged to raise questions, make suggestions, and to carry out various assignments that he or she is willing to accept. The delegation of authority is crucial to an experiential pedagogy.

Chapter Four

Transforming Oppression

AFTER LAYING OUT HIS analysis of the thematic universe and limit-situations of oppressed people's lived experience, Freire turns his attention to their responses to the latter. He dubs these "limit-acts." Such limit-acts are specific ways of working to overcome or remove the fetters that oppressive societies have placed on Third World people. Although Freire does not get concrete as to what these actions should be, he clearly implies that they must involve socio-political acts that work for the liberation of oppressed people everywhere. In chapter four of his book Freire presents the basic emphases comprising the thematic universe of oppressed peoples and then contrasts them to what he considers to be a more real thematic universe that could result from liberating transformation.

Here we shall direct our attention primarily to the possibility of employing this notion of limit-acts to the pedagogy of the oppressor as well. Having explored the thematic universe and limit-situations of the oppressor's worldview in the previous chapter, we are now in a position to reflect on what sort of activity would be appropriate to the transformation of the generative themes comprising the worldview of the First World, especially North America.

Freire offers a specific set of themes which characterize the thematic universe of the privileged world and goes on to suggest how these might be transformed by those working for a liberated society. We can with profit follow Freire's outline as a format for this chapter, while at the same time indicating some of the ways BorderLinks seeks to participate in this trans-formative process with respect to the education of North Americans about the US/Mexico border. Four specific themes and their reversals will be taken up in the following sections of the current chapter.

1. Conquest and Co-operation

The underlying assumption behind Freire's treatment of the major charac-teristics of oppressive societies is the need to distinguish between dialogi-cal, and anti-dialogical modes of behavior. Thus undergirding the desire for and justification of conquest is the refusal to participate in open dialogue with those whom one wishes to oppress. This dynamic is clearly visible in the conquest of the entire what is now misleadingly called "Latin America" by the *conquistadores* of Spain in the 1500s. Throughout its five hundred year history Hispanic America perpetuated its oppressive authoritarian monologue on the indigenous peoples of South and Central America, as well as Mexico. Only recently has this hegemony begun to topple.

The chief method for accomplishing this oppressive regime has been, according to Freire, the "mythicization" process whereby indigenous folks and even the local elites have been led to believe propaganda and false his-tories. Freire describes such myth making in the following way:

> For example, the myth that the oppressive order is a 'free soci-ety'; the myth that all persons are free to work where they wish, that if they don't like their boss they can leave him and look for another job; the myth that this order respects human rights and is therefore worthy of esteem; the myth that anyone who is in-dustrious can become an entrepreneur—worse yet, the myth that the street vendor is as much an entrepreneur as the owner of a large factory; the myth of the universal right of children . . . the myth of the equality of all individuals, when the question: 'Do you know who you are talking to?' is still current among us; the myth of the heroism of the oppressor classes as defenders of 'Western Christian Civilization' against materialist barbarism; the myth of the charity and generosity of the elites, when they really do as a class is to foster selective 'good deeds'; the myth that rebellion is a sin against God; the myth of private property as fundamental to personal human development; the myth of the industriousness of the oppressors and the laziness and dishonesty of the oppressed,

as well as the myth of the natural inferiority of the latter and the superiority of the former. [1]

What is really significant, and scary, about this list of myths with regard to the task of educating North Americans is how many of them actually apply to North America itself. When these beliefs and others like them are internalized by a people they become the very air and life blood of their daily lives, and this is no less true of the oppressor as it is of the oppressed. However, as we have seen, in the former case the process needs to be inverted because here one deals with people who actually are the oppressor but who, for the most part are unaware of, or at least unwilling, to admit it.

The lynchpin of this entire framework of oppression is the refusal to participate in open and egalitarian dialogue with those who are deemed inferior. As Freire insists, it is impossible to have dialogue between unequal partners, for those in the dominant position, the ruling class, have everything to lose and nothing to gain by such procedures. This is why the pedagogy of the oppressor is such a difficult task.

Nevertheless, over the years that BorderLinks has been working on the border the chief reason it has been successful in creating and implementing contexts for real dialogue between North Americans and Mexicans has been the integrity and authenticity of its individual workers. For twenty years BorderLinks staff members, beginning with Rick Ufford-Chase, the founder/director, have built a solid reputation for being people of their word. Things get promised and they get delivered. In addition, the folks with whom they work in Mexico have come to trust both what BorderLinks staff members do and how they do it. Thus they trust them as people and they themselves feel trusted.

Above all, it has always been a BorderLinks policy to involve its Mexican partners in the planning and implementing of its various programs and visitations right from the start. It is this kind of involvement that creates the conditions for genuine dialogue between North Americans and their Mexican counterparts. The families and individuals in Mexico are always asked what and how they think things ought to be done when the different groups come to visit the border, and this incorporation yields the sort of co-operation that is both desirable and necessary for genuine dialogue and understanding.

This brings to mind the advice of Gustavo Gutierrez concerning the most helpful way to accompany the poor. He said that one should spend

1. Freire, *Pedagogy*, 139–40.

significant time with those who are disadvantaged, seek ways to advance the cause of the poor, and be willing to put oneself at risk on behalf of the poor. Being *with* the poor is what BorderLinks has always been about.

It is not difficult to grasp the sort of limit-acts that are appropriate to these oppressive, anti-dialogical limit-situations, whether in relation to the oppressed class or the oppressor class. For Freire activity which establishes and practices genuine dialogue is the key to any transformation of conquest and dominance. So the first step in all revolution and reform is to arrange for real opportunities for open and honest interaction between those whose lives are affected by oppression. For obvious reasons this process must begin with the oppressed themselves, but hopefully it can spread to include members of the oppressor class as well.

This is precisely what BorderLinks has consistently sough to do in its experiential educative endeavors from its very inception. It begins with bringing North Americans to the border to meet and interact with people living and working there. Every opportunity is taken to arrange for such visitors to enter into genuine dialogue with one another, and to reflect on this dialogue with other members of the visiting group.

The chief difficulties here are two. On the one hand, people living on the Mexican side of the border might be apprehensive about such exchanges because they may well view North Americans as oppressors and thus be reluctant to open up to them. By and large BorderLinks has not found this to be a major problem because its Mexican partners have learned to be trustful of whatever BorderLinks arranges. Also, by and large the North American visitors that do choose to visit the border are for the most part sympathetic toward the people and their limit-situations.

On the other hand, since North Americans are indeed the oppressive class in relation to Latin America, they sometimes become either a bit defensive or guilt-ridden when their own culture and country appear in a negative light. It is not easy to acknowledge that one's government and economy endorse policies and practices that exploit and oppress our neighbors to the south. Here again, the BorderLinks staff strives not to stress the individual dimensions of these problems, but rather tries to focus on the general effects and responsibilities which the situation calls to their attention. Neither defensiveness nor guilt are very conducive to transformation.

As was mentioned earlier one of the main concerns of BorderLinks leadership from early on has been called the "So what?" question. In seeking to educate North Americans according to the principles suggested by

Freire, BorderLinks has sought to provide guidance to its participants as to what sorts of actions, limit-acts, might be appropriate to the different specific limit situations they have discerned from their own experience on the border. Such acts must be directed toward changing situations on both local and global levels at home and on the border. These provide possible answers to the "So what?" question.

Some guidance with regard to this question can be learned from what Freire has to say about the transformation of the conquest mode of politics into that of the co-operative mode. Clearly the key here is, of course, dialogue. The place to begin is with the establishment of direct and honest conversations about the issues involved, how they arose and what might be done about them. These conversations can take place on the border or in their home locations. Many delegates actually do become very active in this way once they have returned home, while still others sometimes return to the border to participate in other delegations or conferences.

One young woman who had been a student in the semester program returned to her home high school and gave some talks to various classes there. In the fall, upon returning to her college she arranged to speak in a number of relevant classes about her experience on the border. In addition she now plans to visit other Latin American countries and eventually become a teacher on a reservation near the border. Her story is just one among many, but it is fairly representative. Still, BorderLinks is hoping to do a better job of guiding and following up with the people who have participated in its programs in order to help them answer the "So what?" question.

Since Freire stresses co-operation as the answer to its opposite, namely conquest, it seems fitting to suggest that anyone wishing to transform oppression would find ways to co-operate with others, both individuals and organizations, who are already involved in transformative action. There are a number of groups working all along the border to implement limit-acts trying to help overcome the oppression there. There are, as well many individuals and groups all over North America that are engaged in political action and education aimed at bringing about the transformation of oppression into liberation. These are additional ways to seek answers to the "So what?" question.

On the local level on the border BorderLinks has co-operated with several groups, such as the Humane Borders organization and Derechos Humanos, that seek to provide physical as well as legal aid to people migrating from Mexico to North America in order to find significant paying work. Many of these folks are considered "illegal aliens" by our government, and as such are hunted down, detained, and deported. Many of them suffer a lot in the process, and quite a number have died every year due to the difficulties of crossing the Sonoran Desert. A number of groups are working to get the immigration laws and procedures changed so that those seeking asylum can obtain work permits in the US.

Many people associated with BorderLinks and other like-minded organizations devote a good deal of time trying to influence congress persons to change the entire agenda of our international immigration and economic policies. Freire would surely count these efforts as limit-acts aimed at overcoming the limit-situations faced both by folks along the border and by us North Americans who discover that we ourselves are oppressors. In the immortal words of the cartoon character Pogo: "We have met the enemy and he is us." There are yearly vigils to protest the US government's border policies by a group called No More Deaths. Nearly every year several young people are put on trial by the federal government for having given medical attention to migrants suffering from the dangers of the Sonoran Desert. Here, too, we see examples of Freire's limit-acts.

Unfortunately although the NAFTA agreement has been updated for the better, there still has been little or no progress in immigration reform, especially as it applies to the terrible conditions and bottle-necks at the border between US and Mexico. Things actually got a lot worse during the Trump Administration, and now President Biden has inherited the mess. Hopefully he will be able to improve this obvious sign of first-world oppression, a clear-cut instance of a limit-situation in need of an effective limit-act.

More concretely speaking, there are three other BorderLinks programs that speak directly to Freire's understanding of co-operation as a substitute for conquest. In addition, they all serve to illustrate limit-acts as a means of overcoming limit-situations. The first program involves the sponsorship of international conferences, *encuentros* that focus on specific issues confronting Third World countries, especially those with border tensions and conflicts. The first such gathering centered on the theme of "Economics and Theology" and brought together a number of international scholars and activists for a week-long conference. The conference was held at the Border-Links' Casa Misericordia in Nogales, Mexico and was an excellent example of the sort of co-operative dialogue that Freire speaks of. Several more such bi-national get-togethers are being planned if funding can be found.

The second program is one that offers internships to young people who wish to spend time on the border in order to both learn and serve. These young people will live at the Casa Misericordia in Nogales, Sonora, and lead programs in such things as recreation, English as a second language, and community gardening. In this way these young people will find a way to engage in meaningful limit-acts and thereby help to provide answers to the question "So what?"

Thirdly, more recently BorderLinks has joined with the Catholic Relief Organization of Mexico to provide significant small loans to people living along the border on the Mexican side to start up small businesses of their own in their homes. The hope is that through this program many people will neither have to continue to labor in the *maquiladoras* nor seek to cross the border without papers in order to work in the US. Already several hundred loans have been given out and are also being paid back at a consistent rate. This program holds great promise for the Mexican people, mostly women, living on the border.

2. Division Into Unity

Addressing how oppressors operate in the Third World according to the policy of "Divide and Rule," Freire begins with the following paragraph:

> There is another fundamental dimension of the theory of progressive action which is as old as oppression itself. As the oppressor minority subordinates and dominates the majority, it must divide and keep it divided in order to remain in power. The minority cannot permit itself the luxury of tolerating the unification of the people, which would undoubtedly signify a serious threat to their own hegemony. Accordingly, the oppressors halt, by any method (including violence) any action which even in incipient fashion could awaken the oppressed to the need for unity. Concepts such as unity, organization, and struggle are immediately labeled as dangerous. In fact, of course, they are dangerous—to the oppressors—for their realization is necessary to actions of liberation. [2]

Freire goes on to explore the dynamics of class struggle as perhaps the key instance of the "divide and rule" policy. He makes use of Karl Marx' analysis of class interaction in order to show how the ruling class strives to keep the working class in its subordinate place through divisions of labor

2. Freire, *Pedagogy*, 141.

and levels of management. In the typical factory, for instance, workers almost never see the final product of their labor. Each person has to do only with the particular part of the whole product he or she works with. This not only divides people from people but it also divides people from the product of their labor, thus creating several levels of alienation. That this sort of alienation is counter-productive to human liberation should be more than clear, and Freire offers the following rationale to show just why this is so.

"People are fulfilled only to the extent that they create their world (which is a human world), and create it with their transforming labor. The fulfillment of human-kind as human beings lies, then, in the fulfilment of the world. If for a person to be in the world of work is to be totally dependent, insecure, and permanently threatened—if their work does not belong to them—the person cannot be fulfilled. Work that is not free ceases to be a fulfilling pursuit and becomes an effective means of dehumanization."[3]

An astounding example of this divide and rule policy was presented by the Berlin Council in 1880 where the rulers of a number of European countries gathered to divide up Africa amongst themselves without there being a single African person present. Thus Belgium, France, Germany, England, and Holland all became the "owners" of various parts of Africa and the people living in those respective parts were divided from each other in an extremely artificial way: families from families, tribes from tribes, cultures from cultures.

Another example of Freire's point lies still closer to home regarding the argument about states' rights vs federal rights that surrounded the Civil War. That war was all about dividing and conquering, as all the political squabbles in the ensuing years have been. The southern states sought to control the slaves by keeping them separate as our national government has continually sought to control native peoples by dividing them up onto reservations. Freire argues that a great deal of world politics can be explained by this simple agenda on the part of the "haves" holding it over the "have nots." Especially when the latter can be turned against each other. Divide and conquer has always been the key to keeping oppressed people oppressed.

Clearly one of the major important aspects of this sort of political manipulation is the total individualism upon which it is based. Here again we see the monster of individualistic worldviews raise its ugly head. When one thinks that each person is an independent atom floating in neutral space and connecting with others is optional, then it is natural to conceive of

3. Freire, *Pedagogy*, 145.

unity in terms of free and arbitrary association and the total control of others by whatever means available or necessary.

One way to get a handle on the total pervasiveness of individualism in the North American worldview is by considering the fact that we generally only contrast democracy and totalitarianism as modes of political governance. Indeed, the very concept of governing by consensus, wherein a whole community comes to common agreement concerning an issue or decision, hardly ever even occurs to North Americans. The way of decision making advocated by the Quakers offers a viable alternative to both democracy and totalitarianism. Here the will of the whole group is placed above that of the majority in order to better seek the common good.

Another aspect of our thematic universe which reflects this extreme individualism is our commitment to the notion of private property. In fact, this commitment runs so deep that here again it hardly ever occurs to anyone to imagine any other way of thinking about property and ownership. Nevertheless, the concept of private property is a relatively recent invention in Western culture and did not exist at all in most places outside the West until introduced through imperialist expansion.

In many societies, such as Native American and African societies, for example, all land was shared equally by tribal members in order to enhance the overall well-being of the group. Indeed, when European colonists first tried to buy land from Indian tribes, the latter were quite confused and even considered these white folks to be rather stupid for trying to own and control the earth. Today we ourselves might consider someone who tried to own the sea or the sky as off their rocker, but this may well change as the planet continues to get smaller.

This brings us abruptly to the US/Mexico border where the North American owned *maquiladoras* in Mexico, in conjunction with the Mexican government continue to treat workers as an endless string of replaceable individual cogs in their factories. Unions are legal according to the Mexican constitution, and they exist in some *maquiladoras*, but they are almost all in the pocket of the government, so they do not really serve any real function. Here is yet another instance of what Freire meant by divide and rule. Here is how he puts it: "In order for the oppressed to unite, they must first cut the umbilical cord of magic and myth which binds them to the world of oppression; the unity which links them to each other must be of a different nature. To achieve this indispensable unity the revolutionary process must be, from the beginning *cultural action*. The methods used to achieve the unity of the oppressed will depend on the latter's historical and existential experience within the social structure."[4]

This latter point is relevant to the pedagogy of the oppressor as well. For each person or group must discern and decide which issues and policies they can address and how. No one can fight every battle and all battles cannot be fought at once. Nevertheless, everyone can take some sort of concrete action in order to participate in the transformation of the reality around them. Everyone can engage in some "limit-acts" that respond creatively to some "limit-situations." Every activity that works against individualism and control and toward unity and liberation contributes to the transformation of the world.

Getting specific about how BorderLinks seeks to contribute to this overall transformation by means of its policies, projects, and programs is now in order. The first aspect of this contribution pertains to the bi-national character of the entire BorderLinks organization. Right from the start it was the stated goal of BorderLinks to bring together people from both sides of the US/Mexico border so they would work side-by-side to confront and resolve some of the problems of the lives of those living in this bifurcated region. To be sure, this has not been an easy goal to achieve, but a great deal of progress has been made.

The real breakthrough in this endeavor came when three Mexican Catholic sisters were added to the staff. This brought the total Mexican contingent to five. Shortly thereafter two more Mexican staff members were added, as coordinators of the kitchen, when the Casa Misericordia was acquired, and yet another when the director of Mexican operations was hired. Recently a young Mexican woman was hired as coordinator of housing, and this brought the total of Mexican staff members to eight. There then were twelve North Americans on the staff and all staff meetings were conducted in both English and Spanish. Solid progress has also been made in making the board of directors equally bi-national.

The name "BorderLinks" was in fact chosen in order to focus the organization's commitment to overcoming division and building bridges between the North American and Mexican cultures. Thus, by bringing North American visitors to the border to be involved in experiential education about border issues, the mission of BorderLinks is basically being fulfilled. In addition through its activities at the Casa Misericordia, the organization

---

4. Freire, *Pedagogy*, 175.

is continually working to develop various programs that exemplify this basic bi-national vision of bringing peoples of different cultures together.

A very significant example of this co-operation is the microcredit lending program run in Nogales, Sonora for women in various *colonias*. Several of around a half-dozen women have organized a "banking center" for themselves, following the inspiration of the Grameen Bank of Bangladesh. The women came together and agreed to lend small amounts of money with which to start cottage industry businesses in their homes. As the businesses prospered they repaid their loans, perhaps borrowing again to finance another venture. These women developed small at home factories, quilt making companies, and day care centers for their neighborhoods.

At first it was difficult to convince the women that they could manage such endeavors, because they were basically unfamiliar with dealing with money. In their families the men had always been the ones who dealt with money. But soon their confidence grew and they found that indeed they are capable of such ventures. None of the businesses made a lot of money, but they did allow women to make ends meet while remaining at home with their children. Here again one sees how unity and co-operation can overcome individualism and division. Coming together to plan and work together in this way, having to trust themselves as well as one another, goes a long way toward building the sort of unity that both Freire and Border-Links strive for.

One last example of the way BorderLinks seeks to bring unity out of diversity is found in the makeup of the groups that come to participate in its programs. One major example is that of the semester program, since here the students have the opportunity to return again and again to these central issues in relation to the textbooks and their on-going experience. These students come from a wide variety of locales and backgrounds In addition to the deep and energetic dialogue that regularly arises in this context, there are numerous opportunities for direct limit-acts aimed at transforming their own limiting circumstances, both on the border and at home. It is enriching to see these groups of diverse individuals, working and studying together for three months, emerge as beautifully close-knit community.

3. Manipulation Into Organization

At one place Freire speaks of what he calls another instrument of the overall policy of Division and Conquer involving "pacts" made between the ruling class and those ruled. He puts it this way: "Within certain historical conditions, manipulation is accomplished by means of pacts between the dominant and the dominated classes—pacts which, if considered superficially, might give the impression of a dialogue between the classes. In reality, however, these pacts are not dialogue, because their true objectives are determined by the unequivocal interest of the dominant elites. In the last analysis, pacts are used by the dominators to achieve their own ends."[5]

Freire further argues that the use of manipulation as a technique of oppression only became necessary after the rise of industrialization and its ensuing urbanization, which in turn has led to unionization. The manipulative use of pacts between workers and dominant elites serves to keep the former in line. Every effort is used to keep the dominated class in line, including violence when necessary. He further warns that even the revolutionary leaders and educators may be tempted to employ these methods when frustrated by the oppression they face.

The idea that we North Americans are in fact every bit as imprisoned within our own privileged world-view as are those folks in the Third World in their own oppressive situation is directly related to the three-fold pattern mentioned earlier on as *Ver* (to see), *Pensar* (to think), and *Actuar* (to act). Discovering just what it means to "see" one's own world with some degree of objectivity is what the BorderLinks educational enterprise all about. One way a person can be helped to see his or her own world for what it clearly involves is to place that person in the midst of a different culture. Both while engaged in the different culture and after returning to one's own culture, a person may be able to experience his or her own culture from a fresh perspective.

A practical technique used from time to time by BorderLinks trip leaders is an exercise called Community Mapping. In this exercise participants are asked to construct a map of the community they are visiting, locating important sites such as banks, stores, schools, various kinds of neighborhoods, etc. Then they are asked to make observations about how this layout reflects different aspects of the culture in question. Often this process can be very revealing regarding the political and economic aspects of the society being experienced. It can then prove additionally helpful to have the participants construct a similar map of their own town or city, making some observations about what it reveals, and then comparing and contrasting it with the one they made of the locale they are currently

---

5. Freire, *Pedagogy*, 147.

visiting. Such devises are of great help in facilitating one's ability to see the world, including their own, from a fresh angle.

What needs to be seen by those of us living in oppressing societies is how the ruling class manipulates the oppressed by using what look like progressive measures such as unions, or what Freire calls, pacts. In the context of the US/Mexico border Freire's analysis rings resoundingly true in relation to the NAFTA agreements. These agreements sound as if they would bring US and Mexico closer together economically and socially, but in reality they are precisely what Freire calls a pact that serves the purposes of the dominant class. The only people who really gain from these agreements are North Americans businesses and those who are already well-off in Mexico.

Within our own political system we see the pact manipulation of which Freire speaks in the lobbying activity that literally runs our national legislative process. Fifty years ago it was possible for a not-so-bright high school senior to be surprised to learn that in addition to the three branches that formally control our governmental processes there is a fourth, the lobby system, which actually controls much if not most of the decisions made by our government. The result of the lobby system is that untold pacts are entered into by big businesses, the military, and special interest groups, such as the National Rifle Association, to essentially govern the economic and political decisions of our nation.

Although the idea of organization as an antidote to manipulation may seem counter-intuitive to overcoming oppression, Freire makes a case for understanding this notion within the context of liberation. He contends that organization is directly linked to unity, and is a natural development of that unity. Clearly the sort of organization Freire has in mind must be characterized by qualities contrary to those of a manipulative and oppressive society, but at the same time, any transformation of the reality entrapping those dominated by the oppressive class must have some sort of structure.

At the heart of any effort toward organizational unity, according to Freire, lies a commitment to incorporating the people themselves into the necessary structure. He clearly acknowledges the symbolic power of any effort to join with and incorporate the oppressed in the struggle for liberation and unity. He stresses the need for helping oppressed peoples to learn how to *name* their world, along with helping other peoples to learn to do the same. So it is that the leaders cannot say their word alone, but must say it *with* the people.

One is reminded of the style and example of Subcomandante Marcos the Zapatista leader who systematically insisted on following a dialogical, non-authoritative role as the leader. By so doing he deflated any opposition, both in his own ranks and from the governmental powers that might have sought to overcome the movement. He remained as a faithful witness to the idea of the dialogical liberation of the oppressed people of Chiapas and of all of Mexico. Freire would have been proud of him and his witness.

When it comes to the question of the application of the principles set out by Freire to the vision and programs of the BorderLinks organization on the US/Mexican border, there is much to say. In the beginning there was little need for any serious organization because there were so few people involved and not much diversity of programs. Nevertheless, right from the start serious effort was made to incorporate the Mexican participants into the planning and programming processes.

A number of the initial delegations centered in and around the town of Agua Prieta directly across the border from Douglas, Arizona. Here there were several women of a local parish, along with a couple of Catholic sisters and a semi-radical priest, who were eager to co-operate with this fledgling outfit in the education of North Americans concerning the difficulties faced by those folks living along the border. Not only did these folks open their homes to house and feed their North American visitors, but they went out of their way to participate in the educational dimension of the BorderLinks program through discussions and guided tours of the area and its residents.

This same pattern prevailed when visitors were brought to Nogales, Sonora and eventually to Ciudad Juarez, Chihuahua in Mexico. Here, too, it is appropriate to note that the main reason for the initial success of the BorderLinks organization were the true leadership qualities of its founder Rick Ufford-Chase. That he did and continues to embody the characteristics insisted upon by Freire is attested to by the loyalty he and BorderLinks consistently receive from the various Mexican partners, as well as by the phenomenal growth and qualitative success of the organization. Here is an excellent example of the sort of witness of which Freire speaks.

The dynamics involved in a genuinely liberating organization have also come into play as a result of the very growth and success mentioned above. When there were just a few trip leaders and supporters involved, BorderLinks could afford to be rather loosely structured and articulated. However, when it came to involve over twenty staff and an equal number of board members, as well as a budget that had jumped from about $100,000 to well over $700,000 in a few short years, changes in organization were clearly in order. Delegation of responsibilities became an important organizational factor, but every effort was made not to lose the integrity of consensual participation and input.

Another dimension of the incorporation of dialogical and liberating organization into the BorderLinks programs arises when it comes to planning the agendas for various groups that visit the border. In each case serious effort is made to listen to the wishes and needs of those groups planning to be involved, so as to readily provide valid and viable educational experiences for them. Often, too, changes are made after a group arrives or even during the border visit as a result of input from the participants themselves.

A different sort of example of the need to be genuinely liberating in policy arose during the early days of the first semester program. Having been told that they were to think of themselves as full participants in the nuts and bolts of their own program, the students took BorderLinks at its word and confronted the leadership with a set of suggestions and complaints concerning how the program was being facilitated. As a result, a number, but not all, of the changes the students brought up were incorporated into the program. The same approach was taken with successive groups of semester students. There is little doubt that this flexible process will repeat itself with successive groups.

The really significant point here is that, as Freire so clearly stresses, it is essential that any effort of organization that seeks to be genuinely liberating must be an embodiment of the very principles and values which it hopes to bring about through its actions. Needless to say, the sort of qualities necessary to such transformative endeavors run contrary to those generally taught and practiced by our own North American worldview. Principles that truly empower and liberate oppressed people do not fit with well with the concern to be Number One.

4. Cultural Invasion Into Cultural Synthesis

The final transformation of oppression that Freire considers is shifting from cultural invasion to cultural synthesis. Throughout his discussion he is, of course, speaking about how these transformations can and should take place within an oppressive society divided according to a highly structured class system. Our present situation, on the other hand, is exploring the

possibility of engendering such transformation within the minds and political policies of North Americans. Transforming an entire cultural motif is
what this latter task requires, from cultural invasion to synthesis.

The reality of the cultural invasion perpetrated on the people of what
is now called Latin America by the Spanish conquest in the 1500s was as
thorough as it is well-known. It is almost unbelievable how quickly and
deeply the Spaniards took over and controlled all of Mexico, Central America, as well as the huge continent of South America. Although within the
last two hundred years many of the countries involved in this invasion have
managed to free themselves from European political control, the pervasiveness of the Spanish culture remains.

In the same way, within the same number of years the US, following the notion of Manifest Destiny and the imperialist Monroe Doctrine,
has repeatedly intervened throughout Latin America, sometimes militarily
and sometimes politically, or both. Both types of intervention have usually
been motivated by a desire to protect or extend American business interests. Even these business interests represent the sort of cultural invasion of
which Freire speaks, for they permeate all of Latin America in nearly every
way at the deepest possible level.

The modern, seemingly more subtle modes of cultural invasion generally try to avoid actual military force and violence, but prefer to focus on
economic dominance and implicit political control. However, subsequently
the US became deeply involved in providing military support, training, and
weapons for various Central American governments. Moreover, the US developed a clear record of supporting Latin American dictators. The word
'revolution' seems at times a good word only when used in connection with
our own struggle for independence.

One could spend a great deal of time rehearsing how in recent decades
the United States' cultural patterns have been shaped by an anti-dialogical
virus and has suffered thereby from its consequences. From as far back as
the Nixon administration our government has lied to its people repeatedly
about serious issues and practices. We are continuously being informed
after the fact about atrocities and cover-ups conducted by our government
both at home and abroad. Unfortunately, we generally only learn about
such things years later.

In addition, it is the case that our children have not been provided
with solid educational processes so as to educate and inform them both
about world events and more crucially about the need for a dialogical

approach to learning. This need is not exemplified by our politicians or other cultural leaders, largely because there is little or no public dialogue to be seen either in most homes or in the media. Talk shows are our idea of discussion. Our schools major in socializing rather than educating. At best American educative processes reduce to memorization rather than teaching dialogical and analytical thinking.

Coming to grips with this laundry list of difficulties inherent within our culture of privilege is essential to any pedagogy of the oppressor. For these limit-situations in North American society must be recognized, acknowledged, and overcome before any sort of liberation can take place. We tend to think of our culture as by far the best and above reproach in relation to others. Brandishing our individualism, industry, and belief in the inevitability of progress, will not only not do the job, but such qualities and values may well actually be part of the problem. The fact that our educational system regularly ranks far behind those of many other countries, especially those of the Scandinavian countries, focuses the problem.

Clearly, the cultural synthesis resulting from a cultural revolution will need to embody and be centered in an on-going dialogical process which includes all levels and each member of society, as well as full participation of the populace in the distribution and employment of political power. When Freire speaks of these issues he states: "Joining the oppressed requires going to them and communicating with them. The people must find themselves in the emerging leaders and the latter must find themselves in the people."[6]

In many ways the main emphases of the above quotations from Freire epitomize both the vision and the practice of the BorderLinks organization as it seeks to effect a cultural synthesis on the US/Mexico border. Both in its policies and in its programs BorderLinks has always sought to incorporate and synthesize the knowledge and experience of all of its constituents into whatever tasks it sets out to accomplish. Both at staff and board level great care is taken to listen to everyone's ideas, questions, and objections. This is especially important in a bi-national community made up of folks of one culture that dominates and oppresses the people of the other culture.

One specific way of implementing this commitment to a synthesis of cultures is to honor both of the languages that are spoken by the members of the community, Spanish and English. This is accomplished either through the use of simultaneous translation equipment or by translating each person's comments as they are made. Also, the minutes of staff and

6. Freire, *Pedagogy*, 163.

board meetings are produced in both languages. Sometimes it proves necessary to simply wait for others to gather or express their thoughts, either because this is the polite thing to do or because great wisdom may be in the offing. The ensuing difficulties and time lost are well worth the effort, for in this type of enterprise, people come first.

We North Americans are already so guilty of the cultural invasion of Mexico that it is only right not to brandish our ideas and our solutions whenever a problem arises. To create an authentic bi-national cultural synthesis within an organization seeking to bridge cultures and establish links across the border is as necessary as it is at time difficult. This is why BorderLinks has established two directors, one in Mexico and the other in the US, although the US director actually oversees the entire organization because the vast majority of BorderLinks programs are initiated in the US.

There are some very subtle cultural differences that may go unnoticed by us North Americans, since we are not famous for cultural sensitivity. For example, Mexican folks almost always greet everyone present when they arrive on the scene by giving each person a hug and a kiss on the cheek. North Americans, by contrast, usually just shake a few hands or just say "hello" to everyone at once. Thus when BorderLinks staff gather for a meeting the greetings take several minutes to complete.

One American staff member found it annoying to always have to interrupt what he was doing to get up and go around hugging everyone and saying: "*Como esta?*" over and over again. It finally occurred to him, however, that in order to work for genuine cultural synthesis, and help counteract an already well-established cultural invasion on the part of North Americans, it would behoove him to transcend his minor annoyance and participate in this Mexican way of greeting. The simple fact is that this customary way of greeting is for Mexican people a way of showing respect and care for other persons.

A more difficult cultural issue arose after the Casa Misericordia was acquired and it came time to decide how the Mexican staff members should be paid. On the one hand, it seemed only fair that they be paid the same salary as the North American staff. However, this would result in the Mexican folk actually becoming quite rich in direct comparison to their Mexican neighbors. Finally, it was decided that since the Mexican basic cost of living is about three-quarters that of the US the Mexican staff should be paid three-quarters of what the North Americans receive.

Although this decision was made through full discussion with members of both staffs and directors, it was a very difficult process for the simple reason that in the Mexican culture it is considered extremely rude to discuss financial matters in a public way. Several of the Mexican staff felt very uncomfortable with this whole process, even though they fully realized that it was a decision in which they should participate. Without trying to discern how and why this custom came to be the case, it was clear that creating a cultural synthesis is not as easy as it at first might seem.

By way of bringing this section, as well as the whole chapter, to a conclusion it will be helpful to recall just why these considerations of the transformation of culture are relevant to the pedagogy of the oppressor. The basic overall purpose of the BorderLinks enterprise is to help engender a consciousness and conscience raising experience for those North Americans visiting the US/Mexico border. After having spent several chapters exploring various aspects of this entire educational undertaking, from its paradoxes and dynamics to its specific techniques, it seemed appropriate to devote a chapter to an examination of the goal toward which all of these considerations is aiming.

The rationale for all the foregoing discussions has been the possibility of enabling North Americans, through direct experiential encounter with the realities and people of the border, to come to a first-hand and life transforming understanding of how and why things are this way, and what can be done about it. This is the pedagogy of the oppressor. An effort has been made to follow and apply the principles set out by Paulo Freire with regard to the pedagogy of the oppressed as they apply to the pedagogy of the oppressor. To be sure, not all of these principles apply to this reverse or inverted task of educating the oppressor, but hopefully a sufficient degree of convergence has been articulated to make this plan viable.

Perhaps the most salient feature and intension of this entire undertaking pertains to the importance of BorderLinks, as an educative organization, to embody the very principles it seeks to highlight through its programs and projects. It brings North Americans to the US/Mexico border in order to provide them with experiential education about the realities facing the people living and working there. As part of this process, it seeks to suggest better ways for our culture to relate to its Mexican counterpart. However, if the BorderLinks programs and staff do not embody these same principles and life values very little in the way of transformative education will take place.

In short, it is imperative for the entire BorderLinks operation to ex-emplify the message that it peaches in the way it goes about what it does. This is every bit as crucial as having the right programs and proper contacts along the border. In the final analysis, then, it is the integrity and capacities of those implementing the various BorderLinks endeavors that must make the organization what it us and what it hopes to become. "By their fruits you shall know them."

Chapter Five

Faith Is as Faith Does

ALTHOUGH NEITHER PAULO FREIRE's work in general nor his *Pedagogy of the Oppressed* in particular directly address the question of religious faith, both have been a strong influence on liberation theology, a movement that has revolutionized religious understanding and experience throughout Latin America for over fifty years. In addition, there exist sufficient subtle phrases and intimations throughout his writings to suggest that he himself saw theological issues as central to the task of human liberation and transformation.

In this connection it should not go unmentioned that it was the inspiration that they received from Freire's thought and work that motivated many revolutionary educators within the Catholic church throughout Latin America. The lives and ministries of such church leaders as Archbishop Oscar Romero, Dom Helder Camara, and Bishop Samuel Ruiz in El Salvador, Brazil, and Chiapas, Mexico, respectively render this abundantly clear. In each of these cases, as well as in many more, it was the confluence of Freire's educational philosophy and a theology of liberation that set in motion a veritable revolution in the lives and culture of Latin American Christians over the past sixty years.

It was out of this same confluence that the mission and programs of BorderLinks were born. The insights and radical sacrifices of these church leaders, along with those of Freire, have fundamentally determined the concerns and commitments of the BorderLinks leadership and programs. Thus it should come as no surprise that a thorough treatment of Freire's educational philosophy should conclude with a consideration of the religious corollaries of this philosophy. It also should not go unmentioned that in spite of its religious leanings, BorderLinks has no official connection with any church group or organization.

In any case, religious faith has from the outset played a very significant role in the vision and programs of BorderLinks, and one would be remiss if this dimension of the story of this adventure was left untold. In this final chapter the focus will be on the various aspects of the way BorderLinks has gone about embodying and expressing its faith commitment in the context of its overall mission of experiential education on the US/Mexico border, as well as on the theological basis for this aspect of its enterprise.

1. An Ecumenical Axis

BorderLinks has always characterized itself as a faith based organization, but it has consistently and intentionally left the definition of this phrase rather open-ended. On the one hand, BorderLinks has clearly articulated its commitment to the importance of religious faith in the transformation it seeks to effect among its North American participants. On the other hand, it has always sought not to specify exactly how its various staff and board members interpret what is meant by religious faith. As strange as it might seem, throughout its history BorderLinks has had few if any difficulties arise because of this open-ended posture, either internally or in relation to delegation participants.

When people are signed on as staff or board members they are asked if they are comfortable with this broad understanding of religious faith and are willing to work in harmony with a focus on the Hebrew and Christian scriptures' emphasis on peace and justice as central to the work of Border-Links. Very seldom if ever does someone who has shown interest in working with BorderLinks decide that he or she is not comfortable with this way of understanding religious faith and work. Everyone has agreed with this flexible way of expressing a faith community.

Right from the start BorderLinks has been a thoroughly ecumenical organization, even though its initial support came largely from a specific Protestant church, the Southside Presbyterian Church in Tucson, Arizona. Strong additional support came from a diverse group of believers of Catholic, Lutheran, Disciples of Christ, and Mennonite persuasion. In addition over the years there have been many supporters who affirm no particular religious affiliation at all, though they are eager to work within the Bor-derLinks stated mission. As a line from one of Willie Nelson's songs has it: "There were believers, deceivers, and old in-betweeners," from the very beginning in the BorderLinks organization.

At the deepest level what unites all of these people is a common com-mitment to the peace and justice dimension of the Christian message, a commitment which is shared by people of many faiths. The difficulties on and surrounding the US/Mexico border as well as the causes and possible solutions to these difficulties, unites those associated with the BorderLinks' mission. They seek to help educate North Americans through experiential encounters with the people and conditions along the border, and to thereby raise consciousness and consciences regarding their own role in the reali-ties the people living and working there must face daily.

In their common commitment and task, BorderLinks staff and board are inspired and guided by the lives and work of educators like Paulo Freire. As we have seen, his book *Pedagogy of the Oppressed* expresses many of the points BorderLinks seeks to implement in its work. In addition, the ecumenical axis that stands at the center of this organization's vision and programs makes it possible to integrate its faith-based character with its socio-political agenda: "Faith Is as Faith Does."

The religious makeup of the students who participate in the Bor-derLinks semester on the border program also demonstrates this broad spectrum of approaches to the question of what it means to be faith-based. Over the years there have been a number of students in this program from several Catholic schools, such as Boston College, DePaul University, Holy Cross College, Santa Clara University, and Mount Saint Mary's University. In addition, students have participated from Trinity University, a Presby-terian school, California Lutheran University, and several colleges in the Carolinas of various Baptist and Methodist affiliations.

Even within these standard categories, there has been a wide variety of individuals who represent a rather diverse assortment of belief system. There has been at least one Mormon, an Assembly of God member, an Episcopalian, and a Muslim student in this program. In addition, as was mentioned earlier on, there have been many students in this program who claim no religious affiliation at all.

Finally, it only remains to be said that in its efforts to educate North Americans about the US/Mexico border BorderLinks attempts to incarnate a servant understanding of discipleship, both with respect to the people living on the border and with respect to the North Americans who come to visit. Moreover, BorderLinks also seeks to employ basically indirect methods of education when dealing with this latter group. The idea is not to preach or even teach, but to find ways to allow the people and conditions to speak for themselves.

To some readers this prolonged discussion of the biblical grounding for the BorderLinks mission may seem rather irrelevant. However, it must be remembered that the majority of folks coming to the border as Border-Links delegations already have some knowledge of and commitment to the Christian gospel. Many are from different church congregations, while others are from various theological seminaries and religious colleges. Thus the frequent biblical reflections that are part of the regular BorderLinks agenda turn out to be especially relevant to those in such delegations.

The particular angle of biblical interpretation taken by BorderLinks, and as presented on these pages, may well not be familiar to people in different delegations. Even though not a great deal of time is spent on the interpretive nuances discussed above, in order to provide a thorough introduction to the faith-based character of the BorderLinks enterprise it has seemed advisable to go into such matters in some depth. Hopefully this has, for the most part, proved to be the case.

It should be amply clear from this summary that the BorderLinks version of the term faith-based does not involve any effort to crowd people into a narrow, overly conservative interpretation of religion. With BorderLinks there is no hidden agenda, no attempt to dictate or control anyone's beliefs or practices, as long as they do not directly contradict the commitment to the socio-political dimension of Judeo-Christian faith.

The pages that remain in this final chapter will offer a discussion of the biblical and theological compass by means of which the BorderLinks enterprise seeks to guide its decisions and projects. This compass involves a reconsideration of the nature of the Christian gospel as introduced by Jesus in his inaugural address as recorded in the Gospel of Luke[1] and a fresh interpretation of the notion of the incarnation as a kind of border crossing. All of these topics are directly relevant to the education of North American oppressors.

---

1. Luke 4.

2. A Gospel of Justice

The pivot point around which the Christian faith revolves is the message of Jesus Christ, and thus BorderLinks as a faith based enterprise, however broadly defined, sees itself moving in this orbit. There always have been a wide variety of ways to understand the Christian Gospel, and BorderLinks places itself within this spectrum of interpretations among those who insist on the necessity of exploring the socio-political dimensions of Jesus' teachings. The focus of such interpretations is on the centrality of a concern for justice in these teachings.

A crucial place to begin an exploration of the role that justice plays in the Christian gospel is with the story of Jesus' reading of the Hebrew scripture in his home synagogue in Nazareth, which reads in part: "Jesus opened the scroll and found the passage which says 'The Spirit of the Lord is upon me because he has anointed me; he has sent me to announce good news, to proclaim release for the prisoners and recovery of sight for the blind; to let the broken victims go free, to proclaim the year of the Lord's favor.'"[2]

There is a great deal that needs to be said about this passage in order to draw out all that it implies about the meaning of the Christian gospel. The first thing to be noted is that by and large the actual content of what Jesus says here has been ignored by most of those who profess to believe in the gospel of Christ. It is far more common for Christians to emphasize the fact that in this story Jesus is announcing his divine authority as the one whom God has sent to fulfill the role of the promised Messiah. From there most interpreters may jump quickly to paraphrasing the gospel message in terms of the need to believe in Jesus Christ as one's personal savior.

The fact of the matter is, as the text makes absolutely clear, that Jesus is here announcing the actual content of the message that God has called him to proclaim. To be sure, the issue of his authority to do so arises in this story, but in a sense this issue is best understood as a diversionary tactic on the part of his listeners. For, not only are they put off by the fact that this young man, whom they have known all his life, is now trying to teach them, but they are put off by the message he brings. It has nothing to do with obeying traditional Jewish customs, let alone with anything about saving one's soul in the here and now, or in the life to come.

The passage that Jesus chose to read from is a classic jubilee text, a pointed reminder of the deuteronomic law requiring the Hebrews to

2. Luke 4:17–19.

celebrate the "Sabbath of Sabbaths" when every forty-nine years they were to return all lands to their original owners, cancel all debts, free indentured servants, and meet the needs of the sick and the poor. No wonder the people of Nazareth sought to change the subject by bringing up side issues surrounding by what authority this young upstart had the right to teach them.

The jubilee text is not referring to prisoners in today's sense of the term. Rather, it designates those folks who have been forced into servitude because they have been unable or unwilling to pay their debts, or because they were taken as prisoners of war. When one reviews the facts about the modern prison systems it becomes clear that the majority of people imprisoned in North America, in addition to belonging to a racial minority, are there for crimes that could be better rectified through external guidance and work programs by means of which the offender could actually repay the victim. Such folks are our indentured servants.

When this gospel of justice is applied to the questions surrounding the relations between First and Third World nations it puts us North Americans in a position similar to that of the people of Nazareth. The sorts of issues raised by Jesus in his inaugural message are not those we generally concern ourselves with, either on the national or personal level. What is more, they are not issues that many if not most Christians today see as central to the gospel message. These issues are as troublesome to those in the twenty-first century as they were to the folks in Nazareth of Jesus time.

In spite of all this it should be perfectly clear from this story that Jesus understood his mission as involving radical socio-political implications which cannot be swept away under some sort of convenient spiritualizing interpretive carpet. In this message he is not talking about spiritual prison and release, nor is he talking about spiritual poverty and fulfillment, let alone spiritual blindness and sight. More to the point, he is flat out speaking to the physical and social imbalance and inequity that characterized his own world, and ours as well. In addition, he directly said that he came to fulfill God's promise to set such wrongs right.

In approaching these issues in this way, Jesus was not introducing a brand new gospel. Rather, he was reminding the Jewish people, and the rest of us as well, that these were the same issues addressed by the prophets throughout the Hebrew scriptures. There are, to begin with, the familiar words of Micah: "What does the Lord require of you but to love mercy, practice justice, and walk humbly with your God?"[3] In addition, there is

3. Mic 6:8.

God's scathing denunciation of those who would substitute proper religious practices for taking care of the needy and acting justly in public life: "I hate, I spurn your pilgrim-feasts; I will not delight in your sacred ceremonies ... Let justice roll on like a river and righteousness like an ever-flowing stream."[4]

Although we Christians generally love the majestic tone and universal themes of the prophet Isaiah, we are usually unaware of this prophet's repeated emphasis on the importance of doing justice, and meeting the needs of the poor as a means of worship: "Is not this what I require of you as a fast, to lose the fetters of injustice, to untie the knots of the yoke, to snap every yoke and set free those who have been crushed? Is it not sharing your food with the hungry, taking the homeless poor into your house, clothing the naked when you meet them, and never evading a duty to your kinsfolk?"[5] These words are only a few chapters from the Isaiah's familiar suffering servant passages, chapters fifty through fifty three.

The Gospel of Matthew also frequently focuses Jesus' message in terms of social and political categories which do not always fit with the more traditional and comfortable understanding of his message. In the Sermon on the Mount,[6] which every New Testament scholar agrees contains Jesus' authentic words, Jesus pronounces the blessing of God on the poor, the meek, the peacemakers, the merciful, and the sorrowful, but not on the true believers. Moreover, he praises those "who hunger and thirst after righteousness," yet the vast majority of Christians are unaware that this latter term is perhaps best translated as justice. It is quite clear that Jesus is here speaking in social and political terms.

It is true, to be sure, that there are numerous passages in the New Testament in which Jesus emphasizes more personal qualities and beliefs as crucial to discipleship. The point here is simply that these passages where he stresses socio-political activity as central to the gospel message are far too often ignored or even completely unknown. It is this particular dimension of the Christian gospel that BorderLinks seeks to call attention to, as well as embody, in its vision and programs. In a word, it is not sufficient to focus on personal and spiritual moral qualities in seeking to be faithful to Jesus' message; it is imperative that one does something about the huge inequities between the powerful and rich, on the one hand, and the poor and oppressed, on the other hand.

4. Amos 5:21, 24.
5. Isa 58: 6–8.
6. Matt 5.

Dom Helder Camara, a Brazilian activist bishop, once remarked that when he fed and clothed the poor he was called a saint, but when he asked why there are so many poor, he was called a communist. BorderLinks operates on the assumption that it is part of the gospel message to ask why the conditions, both physical and social, on the US/Mexico border are what they are, who and what is responsible for such exploitation, and what can be done to set things right. Throughout the Bible, from the Exodus, through the Exile, right down to the early Christian community, God has consistently been on the side of those who are oppressed.

In the early Christian community the responsibility to minister to the needs of everyone in an equitable manner was paramount. In the Acts of the Apostles this issue came up several times. The members of the community held everything in common and basically took from everyone according to their ability to share and gave to everyone according to their need.[7] Indeed, Ananias and Sapphira were struck dead as a result of their failure to participate faithfully in the full sharing of their material wealth.[8] Throughout Paul's letter we encounter numerous references to different churches and individuals taking care of the needs of others, including Paul himself, by means of free will offerings and direct gifts.

The letter from James contains perhaps the best known passage concerning the importance of faithfulness in action as the most authentic expression of true faith. "Faith without works is dead."[9] It generally goes unnoticed that it is the same Greek word (pistos) that is translated both as "faith" and "faithfulness," throughout the New Testament. It is this latter translation which most accurately captures the heart of the belief in the Christian gospel, for it indicates that faith, like love, is a way of life rather than some sort of emotion or capacity.

This activist rendering of Christian discipleship is also brought out by paying close attention to the wording of the oft quoted verse: "For God so loved the world that he gave his only son, that whoever believes in him shall not perish but will have eternal life."[10] The Greek word translated "so" in this verse does not indicate how much, in terms of *extent* God loves the world, but rather it designates the *manner* in which God loves, namely by giving what is most valuable for the ultimate well-being of humankind.

7. Acts 2:42–45.

8. Acts 5:1–12.

9. Jas 2:26.

10. John 3:16.

God's love is an action rather than an emotion or disposition. The verse should read: "God loved humankind in this way, or thusly, giving what is most costly on its behalf."

This costly love is seen most clearly in Jesus' life when he, in the words of the author of Philippians, "Humbled himself by taking human form, becoming a servant, even accepting death on a cross."[11] Jesus' *emptying* himself of divine position and prerogatives is truly a radical act and one that it is difficult for believers to accept. For we, like nearly all human beings, prefer that our divinities remain in the heavens, high above our mundane world. Even the writer of this scripture passage goes on to have Jesus *highly exalted* as a reward for having humbled himself. This emphasis on being powerful and victorious over everything is reiterated by the author of the Book of Revelation as well.

A close reading of a crucial passage in John's Gospel, however, reveals that Jesus' servanthood is to be taken far more seriously than one usually imagines. While he and his disciples were gathered for their final meal together, made a special display of washing their feet so as to teach them that the true meaning of discipleship is servanthood. He insisted, despite Peter's protestations, that such acts of serving others are integral to being a follower of "the Way." Here is how Jesus expressed it: "'Do you understand what I have done for you?' he asked. 'You call me "Master" and "Lord" and rightly so, for that is what I am. Then if I, your Lord and Master, have washed your feet, you also ought to wash one another's feet. I have set you an example. You are to do as I have done to you.'"[12]

Admittedly, a large proportion of those who visit the border with BorderLinks may in fact have little familiarity with or interest in the foregoing explanation of the Christian view of God's love in the New Testament. However, it remains true that very many of those who come to the border represent numerous churches and colleges from around the country and they visit the border because of a strong interest in social justice as it pertains to their faith. Thus the foregoing explanation of the religious basis of BorderLinks' concern for justice for the oppressed may well be of special interest to these folks.

Generally speaking Christian people and churches tend to water down these teachings of Jesus so as to reduce a duty to be civil and even generous to toward all others. But Jesus seems to be very clear that this

---

11. Phil 2:7–8.

12. John 13:12–15.

understanding of servanthood is far more radical than traditional interpretations will allow. One must recall that he said something similar in reply to James and John when they asked to be put in places of power and authority when Jesus' full presence is revealed. "The one who would be first among you must make himself last of all and servant of all."[13] This is not just some poetic way of saying that people should be kind to one another. When Jesus says that the last shall be first and the first last, it is his way of saying that the whole business of rank is irrelevant in the presence of God.

The point here is that Jesus himself took this teaching quite seriously and in so doing revealed the true nature of God's character, namely as one who does not need to be first or in a position of power and authority, but who prefers to be the servant of humankind. Indeed, Jesus consistently spoke of himself as the "son of humanity" rather than using royal imagery of himself. This is the real meaning of the name Immanuel, or literally, "God with us." Thus Jesus is the servant savior, the one who gives everything for us.

This whole interpretation of the servanthood understanding of the Christian gospel, even and especially for Jesus himself, is focused in the 15th chapter of the Gospel of John where Jesus presents the allegory of the vine and branches in order to explain how his disciples are related to the master. In the midst of this explanation he says: "This is my commandment: love one another as I have loved you. There is no greater love than this that a man should lay down his life for his friends. You are my friends if you do what I command you. I have called you friends because I have disclosed to you everything that I heard from my Father."[14]

That Jesus' understanding of this radical notion of discipleship as servanthood was limited to interpersonal relationships should be clear from the way Jesus himself acted in relation to the social outcasts and politically marginalized of his own time and place. He consistently approached women, whether respectable or not, as well as gentile dogs, as the Jews were wont to call them, and even rich, oppressive Romans, on an equal footing, while saving his hostile remarks for the pompous and self-righteous religious leaders. Perhaps the most authentic fact of Jesus is that he ate with sinners.

When it came to the education of the oppressors, Jesus relied on parabolic stories that enabled him to create an arena into which the listeners could be drawn and within which they could find a way to face up to the real questions of life. Thus he generally used an indirect method rather than

13. Mark 9:35.
14. John 15:11–15.

a direct one when addressing those in power to allow them the freedom to avoid being defensive or evasive.

3. Crossing Borders

Interacting with the people and conditions on the US/Mexico border may pique one's curiosity about the place of borders in other parts of the world, both now and throughout history. More specifically, if a person considers the Bible to be an important document, he or she might be interested to know just what role borders had in the Hebrew and Christian stories. Surprisingly enough the concept of borders turns out to be quite central in nearly every part of both the Old and New Testaments. Thus it has become crucial in determining BorderLinks' understanding of what it means to be a faith-based organization.

To begin with, it is helpful to reflect on the fact that nearly every story in the Bible revolves around what we today call migrants, refugees, and immigration issues. Right from the beginning, with the story of Adam and Eve, down to the last days of Paul in Rome, biblical characters and events are all about coming and going from one place to another, as well as about the border difficulties in so doing. A brief review of the major stories in the Hebrew and Christian scriptures should make this point very clear.

After the opening chapters of Genesis, which themselves contain quite a number of comings and goings, the Jewish story begins with the wanderings of Abraham from Ur of the Chaldees through Haran to Canaan, down into Egypt and back to Canaan. In almost every case Abraham and his family experienced great cultural displacement when crossing into strange lands. They also had to negotiate with hostile peoples who lied to and cheated them repeatedly. Abraham's sons, Isaac, Jacob, and Esau, all moved around a great deal and were considered outsiders by nearly everyone. The story of Joseph's sojourn in Egypt and of Moses' leading the people out through many hostile tribes to the Promised Land is a familiar tale of perpetual crossing of borders.

It was not long before the kingdom eventually established by Saul, David, and Solomon sub-divided into the northern and southern kingdoms. Each claimed to be the true followers of Abraham and looked upon the other as a nation of aliens. Soon both of these kingdoms were taken into captivity by the Assyrian and Babylonia empires, who transported the captives across many borders to distant lands. Those of the southern kingdom returned to their homeland as strangers and had to rebuild it pretty much from scratch, while those living in the northern kingdom along with still other transplanted people were viewed by the southerners as heretics and half-breeds.

After having been conquered by several different ruling nations, the Hebrew people came under the oppressive rule of the Roman Empire. It was into this situation that Jesus was born, and out of which the first Christian community arose. Jesus himself travelled frequently between his hometown in the north of Palestine and the capitol city of Jerusalem in the south. In doing so he had to pass through the area of Samaria, where a different set of semi-Jewish people lived, ones looked down upon by the Jews as vastly inferior creatures. The Romans, in turn, regarded the Jewish people as backward and peculiar, while the Jews thought of the Romans as imperialist pagans.

The early Christian community spread the message about Jesus throughout the then known Western world, mostly as a result of Paul's missionary journeys. In his travels Paul was able to traverse a great many borders, but he often had difficulty doing so. He, like Jesus, was always on the move, having no place to lay his head other than in the place where he happened to find himself. While Jesus had moved mostly toward the Jewish capitol of Jerusalem, Paul slowly migrated in the direction of Rome, the capitol of the empire.

What is especially significant about all this crossing of borders in the Bible story is that by and large these folks faced the very same sort of difficulties as contemporary people do. The borders that people establish between their own land and the people around them generally are made to keep other people out. Thus, folks who choose or are forced to travel are inevitably regarded as aliens and as a threat to the home country. The hostility generated by this way of looking at things makes it very dangerous for anyone trying to move from one place to another.

In this regard, it should be remembered that both the Jewish and Christian scriptures repeatedly instruct believers not to treat travelers and strangers as enemies, but rather as honored guests. In spite of the fact that very few of the people whom the Hebrews encountered in their wanderings treated them with kindness, the Hebrew people were instructed to remember that they, too, had been exiles in strange lands. Thus they were expected to show kindness and mercy towards those visitors who came into their homeland. The New Testament reiterates these admonitions.

For the most part the Hebrew people were not very kind to those whom they encountered on or around their borders. It was, after all, a war-like time and place in which they lived, with battles being the order of the day. However, they even fought amongst themselves and put great effort into separating themselves from those they deemed unclean or pagan. In the Jewish culture there was a clear-cut class system between rich and poor, as well as between the serious practitioners of the Mosaic Law and those who simply played along.

A major exception to this bifurcated pattern is found in the Book of Ruth, which was probably written as part of an effort to correct the Hebrew people's failure to honor their own teachings about how strangers should be treated. In this story, Naomi goes to Moab with her family when famine comes to the Land of Judah. It should be borne in mind that Moab was a long-time enemy of the Hebrews, so it must have been difficult for Naomi to go there. Naomi's sons who even married Moabite women, later died, as did her own husband. When she decided to return to her homeland, her daughter-in-law, Ruth, chose to go with her.

The significant and beautiful thing about this story is that the Hebrew people not only welcomed Naomi back home, but they fully accepted Ruth, an official enemy, as well. In fact, before long she married one of Naomi's kinsmen, Boaz, and was, as a foreigner, taken into the family and thus became an ancestor of both David and Jesus. It should not be surprising, even though it usually is, to learn that a Moabite woman, a gentile, was part of the lineage of the Jewish Messiah. Such inclusivity was henceforth supposed to characterize the Jewish treatment of aliens.

It is not difficult to transpose all of this to the contemporary scene along the US/Mexico border, beginning with the history of the US invasions throughout Latin America over the last one hundred years, right down to our current border policy. This policy works to guarantee cheap labor for the *maquiladora* industry in Mexico, while driving an increasing number of Mexicans to die trying to cross the scorching desert border in search of better paying jobs. There is very little, if anything, of the story of Ruth in this approach to the needs and hopes of our neighbors south of the border. She was welcomed and they are not.

The socio-political dynamic of border crossing in the Christian scriptures is essentially similar to that found in the Hebrew scriptures. In Jesus' day the Hebrew people were under the thumb of the Romans, but they continued to despise the Samaritans and other gentile dogs as well. Jesus spent considerable effort trying to overcome these hostilities by relating honestly and lovingly to various outcast groups, be they female, gentile, unclean, or even Roman. In this way Jesus sought to cross the borders and barriers between and among those whom he came to serve.

Likewise, his efforts to share the gospel of God's love with people outside of Palestine, Paul worked hard at breaking down and crossing over similar borders and boundaries. Perhaps the most fundamental controversy erupting in the early Christian community had to do with the relationship between Jewish and gentile believers. Many of the former saw their new faith as an extension of their tradition, and thus felt that gentile believers should also become Jewish through being circumcised. Paul and some others maintained, on the other hand, that the gospel of Jesus would not allow for such exclusionary divisions among the members of the community. His letter to the Galatian Christians spells out his position very clearly.

This issue was resolved, at least in theory, at the First General Church Council in Jerusalem as recorded in the book of Acts. There it was concluded that since God plays no favorites, gentile believers are not to be treated as inferior in any way by other members of the Christian community. The effort to establish a barrier between first and second class citizens was officially denounced by Peter, the head of the Christian community in Jerusalem with these words:

> My friends, in the early days, as you yourselves know, God made his choice among you and ordained that from my lips the Gentiles should hear and believe the Gospel. And God, who can read peoples' minds, showed his approval of them by giving the Holy Spirit to them as he did to us. He made no difference between them and us, for he purified their hearts by faith. The why, do you now provoke God by laying on the shoulders of these converts a yoke which neither we nor our fathers were able to bear? No, we believe that it is by the grace of the Lord Jesus that we are saved, and so are they. [15]

Nevertheless this exclusivist strife continued to haunt the early Christian community throughout its early years, and Paul even had to confront Peter himself for his inconsistent behavior toward gentile Christians in a different setting. As Paul put it: "In Christ there is no such thing as Jew and Greek, slave and free, male and female; for you are all one in Christ Jesus."[16]

15. Acts 15:7–11.
16. Gal 3:28.

Unfortunately it took some two thousand years for the other two second-class members of the Christian church mentioned here, namely slaves and women, to even get a hearing on this issue.

All of the above makes it clear that not all borders are geographical. Indeed, the boundaries and barriers that one encounters along the US/Mexico border are more properly to be understood as socio-political and racial rather than as being a matter of space and land. In this way these dividers are similar to those confronting the Hebrew and Christian communities in their respective scriptures. One of the tragic ironies of the border reality is that the people of Mexico are by and large even more faithful to their Christian faith than the majority of North Americans. Nevertheless they are continuously subjected to economic, racial, and political oppression by their Christian neighbors to the north.

The BorderLinks organization seeks to transform these situations in two concrete ways. First, by simply trying to embody the principles and values of authentic religious faith in its dealings with and on behalf of the Mexican people. This comes down to such basic things as striving to be consistent with respect to matters of money and promises, always beginning with the ideas and feelings of Mexicans involved, and supporting the various projects and programs sponsored by those with whom one is working. It also entails being sure that all delegations are led by one Mexican staff member as well as one North American, and that the Spanish language is used exclusively whenever possible.

Secondly, in seeking to transform the conditions on the US/Mexico border, BorderLinks has committed itself to finding as many ways as possible to bring North Americans and Latin American people, especially those of Mexico, together across the borders and barriers that currently separate them. From the standard one to three week trips along and across the border, to the semester on the border program, to the various *encuentro* conferences on border issues, and even to providing internship opportunities for young people from both sides of the border, BorderLinks strives to fulfill its commitment to building bridges and uniting people across borders.

All of the above projects and programs involve the goal of raising consciousness and consciences of North Americans. Since the majority of participants in BorderLinks delegations are in some way or another connected to faith communities, it is possible and wise to make use of biblical stories and themes in the achievement of this goal. People of faith are usually motivated by the lessons of their scripture and so the roles played by borders and barriers in them become especially relevant to matters of consciousness and conscience. Moreover, by incorporating the biblical stories into a consideration of the issues involved on the border, the staff of BorderLinks can fulfill its commitment to approaching such issues indirectly rather than by a preaching or lecturing mode. In this way, the border and the Bible are allowed to speak for themselves.

4. Incarnation and the Poor

There is little doubt that the concept of incarnation is absolutely central in the Christian faith. Literally this idea denotes, as the Gospel of John puts it, divinity "coming into flesh."[17] The heart of Christianity is the belief that, as Paul put it: "God was in Christ reconciling the world unto himself."[18] There are to be sure many different facets to this very rich and significant concept, and the great theologians have explored them down through the ages. Here, however, we shall be concerned with but one aspect of this pivotal notion.

There is a very real sense in which the idea of divinity becoming human functions as a kind of "border crossing" on a cosmic scale. It is revealing to think of Jesus as an alien refugee from another country or world trying to find his way in our world in order to communicate a message of reconciliation. As John expressed it: "He came among his own, but they did not receive him."[19] Or, as Isaiah put it: "He was despised and rejected by humans."[20] Christians generally take the incarnation for granted, even as we North Americans take our right to travel across the border for granted.

Years ago David Bowie starred in a film called "The Man Who Fell to Earth" in which he played a man from a far-away planet who came to earth in order to save his family from dying of thirst on his now barren planet. Although the film eventually went the way of most such films, the opening scenes, which devoid of sound, conveyed a genuine sense of what this experience might have been like, and it provided an opportunity for the viewer to reflect on the psychology involved in the incarnation, to be "a stranger in a strange land."

17. John 1:14.
18. 2 Cor 5:19.
19. John 1:11.
20. Isa 53:3.

Unfortunately, Christians often speak and act as if Jesus was some sort of divine Superman, disguised as a mild-mannered carpenter from Nazareth, who could know everything with his x-ray mind and perform tall miracles in a single bound. The fact is, however, that the gospel accounts simply do not present Jesus in this way, nor did the early Christian community when it labeled such overly imaginative speculations heretical over twenty centuries ago. It is perfectly clear that the Jesus of the New Testament, whatever else he was, was also fully human. He cried, thirsted, got angry and frustrated, and actually died.

In other words, the biblical Jesus of the incarnation really did cross the border between divinity and humanity so that he might effect reconciliation by bringing the two realities together. He became human in order to demonstrate the awesome and radical love of God by the way he lived and died. In so doing he put himself at risk of being misunderstood, persecuted, and even killed. For the most part he actually was misunderstood, by his disciples as well as by his enemies, and ended up as a common criminal, tried, tortured, and crucified.

With respect to his death we Christians often also fail to grasp the full significance of what actually transpired at the crucifixion. Here, too, we generally regard Jesus' death as something like a pretend death in which he knew all along that he would be resurrected in the final scene of the drama. Indeed, many believers are actually quite shocked when informed by the biblical text that Jesus really did die, rather than having simply swooned, and that he really was dead before being resurrected. Not only has the Christian Church consistently claimed that Jesus actually died, but any other view takes all the risk and suffering out of the crucifixion event.

The crucial significance of Jesus' incarnation is that in him divine reality was expressed in a mediated fashion, not in a dualistic manner where divinity was simply superimposed onto or hidden behind his humanity. In the Jesus of the four Gospels divine reality is found in and through his human acts and words, not over and above them. Jesus does not come to earth as a supernatural being, but rather as a fully human person. The secret of the incarnation, then, lies in learning to discern the divine dimension within the human dimension. As Paul reminded us: "Now we see through a glass, darkly, but then face to face."[21]

Thus the truly remarkable thing about the Jesus of the Gospels is not the amazing things he did, but the way in which he went about relating to and

21. 1 Cor 13:12.

liberating people. The quality of his interaction with other people, which to be sure sometimes led to astounding events, is what really set him apart as someone altogether special. Jesus' divinity was not and is not something to be proved but something to be encountered in the integrity of his person. "We beheld his glory, full of grace and truth"[22] not full of fireworks and magic.

Even a brief consideration of the various stories in the Gospels will reveal the unique quality with which Jesus dealt with those with whom he came into contact. Outcast women, tax collectors, blind and lame folks, as well as self-righteous rich people and pompous religious leaders, were all approached in a way that allowed and encouraged them to face themselves, God, and others honestly and receptively. In this humble way, divinity "became flesh and dwelt among us, and we beheld his glory."[23] Perhaps the most striking thing about this incarnational expression of divinity, and yet something that is very often overlooked, is Jesus' strong identification with those who were poor. Liberation theologians, following the lead of Gustavo Gutierrez, have labelled this propensity "the preferential option for the poor." Throughout the Hebrew scripture, from the exodus out of Egypt and the Mosaic Law, right down to the Prophets and the admonitions of the post-exilic restoration, Yahweh consistently took the side of the poor against the rich and powerful. This was no less true of Jesus in the Gospels.

In addition to having very serious reservations concerning the probabilities of rich folk being able to enter into God's full presence (easier for a camel to go through the eye of a needle), Jesus generally confronted the rich with very strong words about their oppressive treatment of poor people. Not only was the rich young ruler rejected because he had failed to look after the needs of the poor, but the rich folk with whom Jesus occasionally dined were chastised for being more concerned about proper etiquette than about genuine hospitality.

By far the most obvious aspect of Jesus' identification with the poor, and again one that frequently gets overlooked, is the simple fact that Jesus himself *chose* to be poor. He left home with very few, he wandered around and stayed with friends, and he had no means of support. Today he would be regarded as peculiar and suspicious at best, and as a vagrant and dangerous at worst. Rather than taking these facts as a vow of poverty, it might be best to take it as an example of how to be *with* the poor, of how to identify with them and their needs.

22. John 1:14.
23. John 1:14.

It must be admitted that those of us living in the highly privileged First World are made uncomfortable by the phrase "preferential option for the poor." It seems to imply that God has preferences, actually preferring poor people to others. A helpful way to avoid this interpretation of the phrase is to emphasize that God's preference is not for the poor per se, but for the option or choice that seeks to rectify the oppression they experience. This, of course, entails a leveling of the playing field, as the saying goes, which will in turn remove the rich from their privileged position.

In his book *On Job* Gutierrez puts it like this: "God has a preferential love for the poor, not because they are necessarily better than others morally or religiously, but simply because they are poor and living in an inhuman situation that is contrary to God's will. The ultimate basis for the privileged position is not in the poor themselves, but in God, in the gratuitousness and universality of God's agapeic love."[24]

In other words, God's love is to be universally shared with all humankind equally, but when conditions exist that in one way or another hinder some folks from receiving the fullness of God's love, these conditions must be removed. God thus prefers, or chooses the course of action that sets about to do so. This is what God did in the story of the Exodus from Egypt. The poor suffering Israelites were liberated from the oppression of the Egyptians, and the Egyptians, of course, experienced this deliverance as an attack on them by God. Those who enjoy the unfair privileged position will have to suffer when justice requires that they give it up.

A very enlightening illustration of the principle involved in this idea of the preferential option for the poor is offered by Roberto S. Goizueta in his important book *Caminemos con Jesus*.

> As a parent of a nine year old daughter and a four year old son, I have at times had to deal with disagreements between them. Since my daughter is much bigger than my son, she has the decided advantage in their fights. When I found her fighting with her brother, how should I have responded? I could have chosen to remain neutral. I might have informed them that since I love both of them equally, I could not takes sides in their conflict. Instead, however, I have chosen to become involved by separating my daughter and her brother. In that context 1) my love was universal and gratuitous, 2) my universal love had to be made manifest concretely in an historical situation, 3) that situation involved injustice and

24. Gutierrez, *On Job*, 94.

conflict (one wrestler was much bigger than the other), therefore,
I had to 'take the side' of my son by separating the children. [25]

Goizueta goes on to conclude that to have remained neutral in this situation would have been tantamount to siding with the larger child, since his inaction would have implicitly condoned the status quo, namely the injustice being experienced by the smaller child. Since the playing field here was already un-level, to take no action, to have no preference, would actually perpetrate and reinforce the current injustice. In like manner, for God to have no preference in such a struggle between the oppressor and the oppressed would be the same as preferring the oppressors. God's grace must seek justice in order to share love universally.

When he continues to explore the concrete implications of the implementation of this commitment to justice for the poor on behalf of God's grace and love, Goizueta stresses the necessity of making this commitment concrete and historical. Thus he reiterates the theme of this section, the relationship between incarnation and the poor. He says: "Because it is an option for particular flesh-and-blood persons, it will also be an option for particular places, the places where the poor live, die and struggle for survival. To 'opt for the poor' is to place ourselves *there,* to *accompany* the poor person in his or her life, death, and struggle for survival."[26] He actually zeros-in on the US/Mexico border when he seeks to make this commitment to the poor concrete.

> For Latinos and Latinas, this form of oppression is also associated in an especially profound way with the borderlands. For a Mexican, transgressing the border is as dangerous as breaching the suburban enclosure. Indeed, what they both have in common is their significance as geographical, spatial instruments of exclusion. A theology grounded in an option for the poor will thus be a theology that is, somehow, born amidst the violence, insecurity, unpredictability, messiness, randomness, and chaos of those *geographical spaces* which function as the most basic and fundamental instruments of exclusion. [27]

The title of Goizueta's book comes forcefully to the fore in its final pages when he insists that to walk with Jesus means to walk with the poor. Like those who travelled in the war-torn countries of El Salvador and Guatemala

25. Goizueta, *Caminemos*, 176.

26. Goizueta, *Caminemos*, 192.

27. Goizueta, *Caminemos*, 200.

accompanying persons threatened with violence, so too must those who would walk with Jesus find ways to accompany, to be with the poor and the oppressed. "To accompany another person is to *walk with* him or her. It is above all by walking with others that we relate to them and love them. This notion now further specifies the act of accompaniment: the paradigmatic form of human action is not simply that of 'being with' another, but, rather, the act of 'walking with the other.' The notion of 'walking–with' incorporates both the ethical-political and the aesthetic dimensions of human praxis."[28]

It should be obvious by now why and how BorderLinks has situated itself on the US/Mexico border in order to fulfill in some small measure the challenge focused so clearly and forcefully by Goizueta's words. By far the best pedagogy is that of providing opportunities for border visitors to experience first-hand the realities constituting border life. In short, what works best is to arrange occasions for North Americans to be able to "walk with" or "accompany," if only briefly, those who are oppressed, and to hope thereby to serve as a catalyst for significant consciousness raising in their minds and hearts.

In concluding this final chapter, as well as the book itself, it is of utmost importance to take note of the final line from a paper written by a student in the BorderLinks semester program. She notes that her new perspective came largely as a result of having been a foreigner. In other words, not only had her consciousness been raised by the simple fact that she had the opportunity to be taken out of her own highly privileged culture for a brief time, but as a foreigner she was put in a position where she could and did learn from people living in an oppressed culture. There simply is no substitute for experiential interaction with the poor if one is seeking to educate oppressors.

Here, then, is the ultimate rationale for the vision and programs of the BorderLinks organization. One educates North Americans about the US/Mexico border by placing them there and allowing them to engage and be engaged by the folks who live there. All of this takes us back to the principles set out by Paulo Freire in *Pedagogy of the Oppressed*. Not only do the oppressed have to educate and liberate themselves, but the oppressors, as well, must be educated and liberated by those whom they oppress. In the end, BorderLinks works because it relies on the educative powers of its Mexican partners, those who actually live, struggle, and too often die on the border.

---

28. Goizueta, *Caminemos*, 206.

Conclusion

Hope and/or Realism

As I shared earlier, on one of the regular BorderLinks delegations a group of about twenty were having dinner prepared by Doña Ramona in her dirt floor, candle-lit living room in a typical *colonia* in Nogales, Sonora. After Ramona had shared the realities of her life as a *maquiladora* worker with several live-in daughters and grand-children, one of the visitors asked her what gives her hope. She paused for a moment and then replied: "Hope is a luxury I must do without. I just get up every morning and go to work." The stunned silence that followed this remark was deafening.

We North Americans are so optimistic and progressive in our outlook that we have a great deal of difficulty understanding how anyone can live without hope. After all, since we have the power and freedom to do something about our basic situation, be it ever so negative we cannot help but assume that everyone has the same opportunity. To simply put one foot in front of the other day after day strikes us as a kind of living death, and well it might, since this is the way a great many people in the Third World experience their lives, as a living death.

This particular issue brings to mind the age-old theological controversy over whether God's full presence will be realized progressively or completely, all at once, from beyond history. When applied to issues of justice and oppression, this abstract debate becomes much more concrete. Put bluntly, the question is: Will the transformation at which liberation theologians and political activists aim be realized from within history or must we wait for God to bring it to us from beyond history?

This issue, which is often defined as a debate over whether there is reason to hope and work that God's full peace and justice will eventually prevail in this world, or whether realistically speaking we shall have to wait for "the new heaven and new earth," will not unsurprisingly be resolved on these pages. However, the point/counterpoint this issue focuses poses the two relevant, but very different, postures of hope and realism. People who take up the former posture are sometimes called idealists, while those who strike the latter are often called pessimists. How does this debate relate to the prospect of educating the oppressor in general and to the endeavors of BorderLinks in particular?

There might be some sort of mediating position between these two standard approaches to the realism versus hope debate that would apply to both of the above questions. Often thinkers who wrestle with these issues propose a compromise that acknowledges the partial presence of God's grace and justice in the here and now, while looking forward to their final fulfillment. However, such 50/50 compromises generally leave everyone involved less than satisfied. Paulo Freire himself never seemed to come down on either side of this issue. He always talked and acted as if there is real hope for the fulfillment of the world's transformation within history. At the same time, however, he was not naïve about the depth and extent of the oppression dominating much of the world. He believed in and worked for change, but he also knew that those who labor in this field must be in it for the long haul.

As far as BorderLinks is concerned, the best answer to this question comes in terms of the notion of integrity. The work of educating the oppressors, like any work that aims at transformation, has to be seen as an end-in-itself. In other words, it has be as Plato said about virtue, it is its own reward. That is to say, those working for change along the US/Mexico border must do so for the work's own sake, rather than because they believe that it will soon, or even ever, "pay off." Peace and justice, like grace, love, and faith, carry with them concrete values and enrichments which render the actions undertaken on their behalf of intrinsic worth.

So integrity is the watchword throughout the programs, projects, and processes engendered by BorderLinks. Specifically, this means that even though little time may be devoted to evaluating the long-range goals and prospects of the organization in relation to any actual progress or improvement with respect to the difficulties faced by those folks living on the border, there is continual energy and attention given to making each and every decision, conversation, and relationship embody a spirit of reflective integrity.

Bibliography

Austin, J. L. *How to Do Things with Words.* Cambridge, MA: Harvard University Press, 1962.

Berger, Peter. *Pyramids of Sacrifice.* New York: Basic, 1974.

De Tocqueville, Alexis. *Democracy in America.* New York: Alfred A. Knopf, 1945.

Dewey, John. *The Quest for Certainty.* New York: Putnam and Sons, 1960.

Fanon, Franz. *The Wretched of the Earth.* Paris, France: Francois Maspero, 1961.

Freire, Paolo. *Pedagogy of the Oppressed.* New York: Continuum, 2000.

Galbraith, John Kenneth. *The Acquisitive Society.* New York: Houghton and Mifflin, 1958.

Goizueta, Roberto S. *Caminemos con Jesus.* New York: Orbis, 1995.

Gutierrez, Gustavo. *A Theology of Liberation.* New York: Barnes and Noble, 1972.

———. *On Job.* New York: Orbis, 1987.

Marx, Karl. *Economic and Philosophic Manuscripts of 1844.* Moscow: Foreign Language, 1961.

McCann, Dennis. *Christian Realism and Liberation Theology.* New York: Orbis, 1981.

Sartre, Jean Paul. *Existentialism Is a Humanism.* New York: Philosophical Library, 1957.

Soros, George. *The Crisis of Global Capitalism.* New York: Barnes and Noble, 1998.

The New English Bible. Oxford University Press, 1976.

Index

www.ingramcontent.com/pod-product-compliance
Lightning Source LLC
Chambersburg PA
CBHW071132280326
41935CB00010B/1191